The Professional Pet Sitter

Your Guide to Starting and Operating a Successful Service

Lori and Scott Mangold

Paws-itive Press®
Portland, Oregon

The Professional Pet Sitter

Your Guide to Starting and Operating a Successful Service

By Lori and Scott Mangold

Published by: **Paws-itive Press®**
Post Office Box 19911
Portland, OR 97280-0911
(503) 452-9699; (800) PET BOOK
Fax: (503) 452-0858

ISBN Number: 0-9635442-1-7

Library of Congress Catalog Number 92-94300

Copyright ©1991, 1994, 1999 Kitty and Home Services, Inc.
First Printing 1994
Second Printing 1994
Third Printing 1995, revised
Fourth Printing 1999, revised
Fifth Printing 2000

DISCLAIMER

This guide is designed to provide information in regard to the subject matter covered. It is sold with the understanding that the publisher and authors are not engaged in rendering legal, accounting or other professional services. If legal or other expert assistance is required, the services of a competent professional should be sought.

Every effort has been made to make this guide as complete and accurate as possible. However, there may be mistakes both typographical and in content. Therefore, this text should be used only as a general guide and not as the ultimate source of pet sitting information. Furthermore, this guide contains information on pet sitting only up to the printing date.

The purpose of this guide is to educate and entertain. The authors and Pawsitive Press® shall have neither liability nor responsibility to any person or entity with respect to any loss or damage caused, or alleged to be caused, directly or indirectly, by the information contained in this book.

PREFACE

The American lifestyle is changing. Men and women, today, are giving more of themselves to their busy professional lives. They work longer hours, postpone having families and frantically cram vacations into what little leisure time they can arrange. For affection, they have pets. They adore their pets, even though they often conflict with business and pleasure travel. Unfortunately, peoples' busy schedules limit having close friends or knowing neighbors who can care for their pets while they're away. That's where pet sitting comes in -- providing care for pets in their own homes.

Pet sitting has been around for years, but pet owners' busier schedules, now, and increasing dependence upon professional services are propelling its popularity. Business publications refer to pet sitting opportunities ("The Kiplinger Washington Letter", August 30, 1991, page 3). It may be the opportunity you've sought -- for income, to run your own business and to enjoy what you're doing. It certainly has been that for us, and we'd like to share it with you.

We are Lori and Scott Mangold, professional pet sitters. Lori is President of Paws for Awhile, a successful kitty sitting and home services business in Portland, Oregon. Scott is her official helper. In recent years, many would-be pet sitters have watched us and asked our help in getting started. We're proud of our systems, quality service and successes. We believe we can make a significant contribution to the profession and to pet owners by helping other pet sitters.

The Professional Pet Sitter is intended to guide you in starting your own business. Because we're targeting a specific service -- pet sitting -- *The Professional Pet Sitter* won't be as broad as are many books on starting new businesses. But it will be pertinent, addressing how we organized Paws for Awhile and reflecting the many lessons we learned along the way. We won't tell you how to give pills, walk dogs or clean bird cages. Since you love animals, we'll assume you have those skills.

The Professional Pet Sitter may not tell you everything you'd like to hear. If, for instance, you think you'd like to hire a large work force right away, we won't encourage you. As we'll explain, we think that's not the way to begin. We will guide you through what we believe is a more reasonable way to start and establish your business. We'll take you through it by-the-numbers. You needn't follow our advice exactly; in fact, we encourage you to modify our procedures to suit you. As you read, you'll find that we stress planning, organization, disciplined consistency and highest-quality service.

An important goal for you should be having some fun. The opportunity to do that is why many people give up corporate careers to be pet sitters. Running our business, where we control quality, has been very rewarding. We'd like you to enjoy the profession as much as we do.

CONTENTS

	PAGE
1. INTRODUCTION	1
What is "Pet Sitting?"	1
"Why Am I Doing This?!"	3
2. INITIAL ORGANIZATION -- GETTING STARTED	7
Basic Decisions	7
Other Legal Requirements	14
Insurance	17
Setting Up Your Office	18
3. MARKETING	25
What is "Marketing?"	25
Refining Your Services	26
Marketing Tools	34
Introductions	37
Marketing Beyond Introductions	40
4. DAY-TO-DAY ORGANIZATION -- RUNNING THE BUSINESS	43
Need for a "Routine"	43
Daily Routine	46
Month-End Routine	72
Year-End Routine	73
5. PROVIDING SERVICE	75
What is "Service?"	75
The Basic Service Routine	76
Ah, Success!	84
Summary	86
6. PITFALLS AND ADJUSTMENTS	87
"Why the Negatives?"	87
More About Help	88
"Other Pet Sitters?!"	88
Other Pitfalls	89
PROFESSIONAL PET SITTER FORMS	93

ILLUSTRATIONS

FIGURE   **PAGE**

  1 Desk Pad Calendar   47
  2 4 x 6 Client Card   48
  3 Monthly Schedule   50
  4 Service Agreement   52
  5 Daily Schedule   55
  6 Daily Report   57
  7 Time Sheet   59
  8 Expense Report   60
  9 Money Receipt Book   62
10 Reconciled Daily Report   65
11 Deposit Receipt   66
12 Monthly Accounting Report   67, 68, 69
13 Monthly Accounting Report Showing Expense Checks   70
14 Posting of Deposit Which Includes Expense Reimbursement   70

1

Introduction

What is "Pet Sitting?"

Years ago when we were kids, if the family ever vacationed, the dog would go to a kennel, and neighbor kids would feed the cat, bring in the mail and -- hopefully -- do some watering on hot days. There weren't many burglaries, then, so not much consideration was given to security. And not much went wrong. Buster occasionally brought home fleas, plants were over- or under-watered, and Fluff ignored us for several days, but the system worked okay. After all, we didn't leave home much in those days, and they were only plants and animals, anyway. No one ever heard of professional pet sitters!

Times have changed, haven't they? American society, today, is much "higher tech." People work longer and play harder. They leave home often, traveling tens, hundreds of thousands of miles on business and pleasure. Having values and goals different from those of past generations, young couples today often postpone or forego having families. They -- and an increasing number of single adults -- turn to pets for affection. But these aren't back-yard dogs, barn cats or the often-ignored animals we called "pets" when we were kids. Instead, they're highly pampered and well cared for, often treated like children. They're a very important emotional part of their owners' lives.

Times have changed

Traveler anxieties...

In today's society, how are pets cared for when their owners travel? That can be a problem for a number of reasons:

- We're more aware than we used to be of trauma animals can experience when removed from their loving homes and familiar environs.

- We're more critical of the care quality our pets receive.

With frightening increases in crime, another anxiety travelers have, beyond their pets' welfare, is leaving the home an unattended target for burglary. One solution to both problems is to find someone to live in the home and care for the pets while owners are away, but live-ins can present problems, too. How about the neighbors? Today, as the corporations we work for move us around the country, we tend to live away from families and friends, and we rarely know the neighbors well enough to ask for or trust their care of our pets and home.

The Professional Pet Sitter

And so enters The Professional Pet Sitter!

What is a "pet sitter?" Someone who, by agreement and for fee, goes to a traveler's home, provides basic and specified pet care, basic home security and anything else which he/she and the client have agreed to. The pet sitter may define and offer any services he chooses: some provide yard card, others clean homes. Some care for all animals, others only cats, for example.

Grandma would say it's preposterous to pay someone to feed Buster and Fluff! But pet sitters do far more than that. They provide companionship, love and home care. And Grandma, look at the home services people pay for, today, in order to squeeze a little leisure time into busy professional schedules: gardening, housekeeping, window washing, pool maintenance, indoor plant care - even catering of each night's dinner!

The professional pet sitter provides loving care and peace-of-mind. And busy people today, traveling for business or pleasure, are willing to pay commensurately for that important peace-of-mind.

"Why Am I Doing This?!"

Here is some of the most important advice we'll offer you: your first steps to becoming successful are analyzing why you want to become a pet sitter, deciding that your reasons are good ones, then remembering your motives as you do business.

Our most important advice

Does this seem silly? Not when you consider that motives often are the difference between success and failure. Think of the people you've known who hate their work, lose businesses or keep changing jobs. In every case, they should have been doing something else. Teachers -- good ones -- are motivated, not by a desire for long summer vacations, but by their love of communicating knowledge, imparting values and maybe making the world a better place. Successful travel agents aren't just looking for travel discounts; they enjoy computer analyses, time pressures and selling.

"Why the lecture? I know why I want to pet-sit: there's good money in it. Anything wrong with that?"

Heck no! The profit motive is fundamental to capitalism. It's a great reason to start a service. But it's not enough. It can't be your only reason or even your overwhelming motive. Why not?

We've recently watched a couple of pet sitters fail, in part, because they didn't project a love of animals. Perhaps you can paint houses without loving the work, but you can't successfully pet sit without the animals' confidence or that of their owners. Why?

You have to love animals

• Clients want you to love their "little ones" as much as they do. Otherwise, how can they trust you to provide the care they specify? (This is a reason we became pet sitters: we were convinced no one could provide the loving care our pets need.)

• Try finding, then giving medication to a cat who doesn't trust you!

If you want jobs and to be asked back again, then you've got to show that you love animals. I suspect that a number of would-be pet sitters have discovered that you can't pretend love. Perhaps some owners can be fooled, but not their pets. Animals know.

"Okay, I love animals, and I show it. Aren't that and the profit motive enough reasons to be a pet sitter?"

No, they're not. Consider how you feel about running a business.

"Running a business? Whoa! I'm talking about walking dogs, cleaning litter boxes and bringing in the mail, not being Chairman of General Motors!"

Pet sitting is a business

Calm down! After it's organized and functioning, you can run a small business in a few minutes each day. What we're saying is, there are many aspects to any service, and they require attention and coordination. To be a successful pet sitter, you must conduct your service as the business which it is. All around your service calls, you're going to be planning, purchasing supplies, marketing, taking reservations and accounting for all you do. That takes organization. The time, effort and skills you put into keeping your pet sitting service organized constitute a "business," in one form or another. More about this, later.

Whether you fantasize that you're the Chairman of General Motors or you put in minimal "office" time each day, you truly can enjoy running your own small business. To begin, you don't need training or special skills, just an interest and willingness to learn. You will find your skills developing as you organize and tend your business. As your systems fall together and your business grows, so does your enthusiasm. It's exciting to run your own business!

A corollary of having your own business is being your own boss. If you've worked for others for 20-25 years as we have, being your own boss has special appeal. Have you ever heard the boss use you as a scapegoat for his mistakes? "Well, I told my girl to mail it to you" or "He wasn't following my instructions." On the other hand, as your own boss, you bear responsibility, but you also have authority to make decisions and control over what happens.

Part of what happens is the quality of your service. Will it be consistently-high quality? One of the frustrations of working for a big company is the individual's inability to affect quality very much. If you're one of 1000 employees making widgets, there's probably not much you can do to eliminate a 15% defect ratio. On the other hand, if you run a small business -- if you're the boss -- then you control quality. We're able to say, at time of writing, that we've never had a complaint in our pet sitting business. That and the praise and gratitude we've received are strong motivation for being pet sitters!

These: profit motive, love of animals and desire to run your own business (which includes being your own boss and controlling quality) certainly are not the only "correct" reasons to be a pet sitter, but they're good ones. They've motivated us. But there's one more reason, really a part of loving animals or of wanting to run your own business. Or perhaps it ought to be considered as a general theme: the desire to have some fun. Considering how many people die wealthy but miserable, maybe a large measure of "success" is whether it was fun getting there. What we know for sure is, given the opportunity to make a little money while enjoying the work -- having fun -- we'll take it over any other. We think that opportunity is pet sitting.

Motivations

"What am I missing? Why the exercise in identifying correct reasons for wanting to be a pet sitter?"

Because we want you to remember them, every day. They're your motivation. It's your motivation which will lead you through the frustrations you'll encounter. When nervously driving icy streets to complete a high number of visits on Christmas Day, we want you to remember the love of those animals, the gratitude of their owners and the revenue opportunity of the busy, hectic times of the year. When you're discouraged with light bookings during February, we want you to think like General Motors' Chairman and motivate your marketing department into gear (that's also you).

Staying motivated

A poster in a friend's corporate office reads, "I keep forgetting -- tell me again why I like this job so much." If you're ambitious enough to start your own business, you should never have to ask yourself in time of frustration, "Why am I doing this?!" Remember your reasons every day -- keep your motivation in sight and your business on track.

2

Getting Started

Basic Decisions

You've decided you want to be a pet sitter. You've considered your reasons, and they're sound. Getting started, now, will require some organizing: it's time to put together your business.

We call your service a "business," because there will be more to it than just caring for animals. You'll be supporting your service calls with a lot of planning, marketing, coordinating and accounting. You'll face many decisions, and you need a framework within which to make them. That framework is your business.

A decision framework

"Business" is a nebulous term. To see what yours will look like, you must begin with important BASIC DECISIONS about your services, who will help and how things will get done.

The starting point is to DEFINE YOUR SERVICES, deciding what you will and won't do. How broad, how narrow will your range of services be? Can you care for large animals like horses and livestock? How about "exotic" animals -- are you afraid of reptiles or rodents? It's amazing what kinds of pets people have! Maybe you'll want to specialize in those animals you prefer, like cats.

Services to offer

Which non-pet or "home" services will you offer? Basic security generally is simple: bringing in newspapers and mail, changing lights and window blinds. Indoor (and outdoor) walk-arounds, patrolling for accidents, damage and hazards are a good idea.

What other indoor services will you offer? Will you limit your cleaning just to kitchen counter top and those areas the animals occupy? Some pet sitters offer light housecleaning and even laundry services. You'll offer to water indoor plants -- unless the client's home resembles an arboretum!

How about other services? You'll probably offer to water potted plants on the deck, but how about yard shrubs, the garden and the lawn? Some pet sitters advertise lawn mowing and yard care. If you do, too, will you use clients' tools or your own?

There are some tough decisions in defining your services. First, you must weigh your skills and interests. Remember your reasons for being a pet sitter -- if you love animals, you may not want to stray too far into housecleaning or yard work.

Geography dictates part of your service

Consider the geographic areas you'll service and those clients' probable needs. How broad a range of services will you have to offer to attract business? If you'll serve just a downtown or high-rise area, you can forget about yard care. Your clients will have cats, small animals and houseplants. If, on the other hand, you live in a rural area, give thought to livestock -- before you begin getting inquiries.

Consider the special needs of some animals and the time those services will require. Are you willing to spend, say, two hours with livestock or mowing a lawn when, alternately, you could complete two cat or dog visits? Part of the answer involves enjoyment, and part considers money -- how much revenue can you realize from different services? Some pet sitters avoid jobs which require walking a dog twice a day, because, after a two-visit-per-day discount, the work is too demanding. Others, however, do "daily doubles," but, recognizing the value of their time, they avoid the discounts and charge for "extra" services, such as walking dogs.

DWYDDW

An important consideration in defining your range of services is quality. Don't over-extend yourself; remember DWYDDW: "do what you do do well." If you have a "black thumb" -- you're notorious for overwatering and killing plants -- limit your plant care (or ask clients for precise instructions). If you're not crazy about some creatures, ask the client if maybe a neighbor child might enjoy the alligator and tarantula while he travels. If you try something you're unprepared for or not good at, quality won't happen. In fact, the results could be disastrous! DWYDDW.

So that there will be no misunderstanding, disappointment or disputes, later, communicate clearly what your services include and exclude. Your marketing need not address alligators and tarantulas, but be sure you're tactfully explicit in your conversations and service agreements.

Be explicit

Having decided which services to offer, your next basic decisions involve HELP. Do you need it? Perhaps you can handle everything, initially, but as your business grows, will you need help? Who will provide it?

Will you need help?

To answer these questions, first consider the activities your business will involve: running it, marketing and making service calls. Do you have time, each day, to be manager and service person, or are there other demands on your time, like being a parent or having another job? Can your spouse help out? More importantly, do you <u>want</u> your spouse involved in your business? Give that question long, hard thought. He or she may be able to provide needed skills or man-hours, but what will working together -- being together all that extra time -- do to your friendship?

Maybe you have a partner in mind. Again, he's a source of skills and man-hours, and you think you'd really enjoy working with him. But consider control. On one hand, it might be nice to share decision-making with a partner, but on the other, if he's opinionated or forceful, you might find yourself excluded from important decisions. The business could begin moving in directions you can't control. Another potential problem with having partners is that you're usually liable for their actions. Can you trust your partner?

How about hiring employees? We suggest you give this long thought after discussing it with an accountant and attorney. We'll talk about having employees later in this section; for now, we just want to introduce the idea. To us, the question of whether or not to hire involves deciding if we can afford employees, financially and in terms of service quality. If you sense that we have strong inclinations, you're right. Corporate supervisors for many years, we've each taken our share of sick calls and customer complaints. Employees can give you needed man-hours, but they also require time to administer and supervise. If you envision a large pet-sitting empire, then you'll need employees. Otherwise, perhaps not.

Professional help

One source of help -- not everyday, but very important -- is professional help. We suggested you discuss the employment issue with an accountant and attorney. The periodic guidance of professionals, specialists in legal areas affecting your business, can keep it moving in the right directions. You'll need an accountant and an attorney to help you choose the best legal structure for your business (which we'll discuss as your next basic decision), then, perhaps, to set it up. How do you select the right professionals? Seek recommendations from friends and other small businesses. Give special consideration to those who specialize in small service businesses in your area. Then interview several. Assess their strengths and interests. Do they seem interested in you and your new business? Ask and compare their fees. The old adage, "You get what you pay for," doesn't necessarily hold true -- you don't have to pay a fortune for the accountant and attorney who meet your business needs.

Another professional to locate is a reputable, independent insurance agent or broker. Before you begin service, you'll need adequate liability insurance. Then, if you elect to hire employees, you'll need a bond and workers' compensation insurance. An insurance agent who knows you and your business can arrange adequate insurance at reasonable or competitive rates.

If you do opt for help in your pet sitting business, it's important to define roles. Certainly, you can agree to changes, later, but to begin working together smoothly, you and your spouse, partner or employee(s) must agree on authority, responsibilities and who will do what. You should strive for a realistic division of labor, based on skills, strengths, interests and time available. Consider who has other obligations (e.g., jobs, family responsibilities). To insure that you've defined roles correctly, discuss your expectations of one another. "Oh, I thought you were doing my expense reports!" exposes an unrealistic expectation, based on inadequate discussion of roles. (Take our word for it -- this is particularly important when spouses are involved in a business!) The division of labor which works well for us is:

- Lori: marketing, reservations and service.

- Scott: (who has another job) bookkeeping, peak period service assistance and emergency backup.

- Lori and Scott: all planning and critiquing.

Another reason for considering help -- beyond answering the question, "How am I gonna <u>do</u> all this?!" -- is that, who else is involved in your business will have a bearing on your next basic decision: what LEGAL STRUCTURE your business will take.

The legal structures which small businesses commonly take are "sole proprietorship," "partnership" and "corporation." Why is legal structure important? Because it defines ownership and -- where more than one person is involved in a business -- relationships, authority, control, responsibility and distribution of profits or losses. If you'll include others in your business, but wish to retain authority to make important decisions, then you'd better plan to operate as a sole proprietorship. If you're concerned about responsibility for coworkers' errors or bad decisions, then you may want to incorporate to limit your liability. Also, your legal structure and how you're compensated will affect your income taxes, business and personal. Let's look briefly at these legal structures.

Legal structure options

The <u>sole proprietorship</u> is the legal structure probably most used by small businesses. If you operate as a sole proprietorship, you own the business. In fact, you <u>are</u> the business, whether you work alone or have employees. That is, you have total authority and control, unless you delegate to employees. Correspondingly, you're totally responsible for what happens; you can't avoid liability. All profits or losses from the business pass over to your personal income tax returns; the business doesn't file a return or pay taxes. If you have no employees, the business needn't apply for a federal identification number. Note the one exception to the sole ownership feature: in community property states, a sole proprietor's spouse is deemed to have a half interest in the business.

Sole proprietorship

The sole proprietorship's biggest advantage is that it is the simplest form and easiest to set up. You needn't file any applications with government agencies, so you waste no time awaiting approvals. Bureaucracy is minimal. Usually, a sole proprietorship needs only business licenses to operate (although some states may require them to register). If you do nothing to formalize another legal form, then you become, in fact, a sole proprietorship.

The primary disadvantage of a sole proprietorship is the owner's unlimited liability in the event of damages, lawsuit or other financial losses. In weighing this risk, the sole proprietor must consider his services, losses which they might cause and the extent of his personal assets. What does he risk losing?

Partnership

A partnership is like a sole proprietorship which has two or more owners. Partners share authority, control, responsibility and profits or losses. By agreement, partners are "equal" or "unequal," based on what they contribute and draw out of the business. Each is an "agent" for the business and is liable for the actions and debts of the other partner(s).

A partnership isn't difficult to set up. Like a sole proprietorship, it normally requires no government applications, just business licenses (but verify with your state). What is very important, though, is that partners have a formal agreement which defines the contribution (e.g., capital, time), authority, control and reward of each.

Taxes are only slightly more complicated than with a sole proprietorship. Profits or losses still pass over to partners' individual income tax returns. Partnerships must apply for federal identification numbers and file federal and (usually) state informational returns, not to pay taxes, but to report each partner's profit or loss.

The advantages which a partnership can offer are additional resources (including man-hours), skills, knowledge, good judgement and companionship. In a seven-day-a-week business like pet sitting, the man-hours can be important to you. But there are disadvantages, and they aren't unlike those challenges of a marriage. Can you maintain a relationship with your partner(s) in which you amiably share responsibility, control and profits? Will you trust one another's judgement, commitment and contribution? Are you willing to be responsible for your partners' actions and debts, to the extent of your personal assets? In some instances, you can be held liable for even your partners' activities outside the partnership. Liability must be a big consideration.

The third legal structure, the <u>corporation</u>, is an entity, a living being, separate from its owners. A corporation must be chartered to do business by a state. Its "owners" are the stockholders. They contribute capital by buying ownership certificates, or stock, and the corporation compensates them by distributing dividends, a portion of profits. The stockholders elect a board of directors to guide the corporation and protect their interests. The directors, in turn, elect officers to run the corporation's day-to-day business. In this way, the owners delegate authority and control to the officers, and the officers and directors are responsible to the stockholders.

Corporation

The big difference between corporations, on one hand, and sole proprietorships and partnerships is that, as entities, corporations are liable for their debts. This means that officers and directors are responsible for their actions to the extent that they can be fired or not re-elected, but generally, their liability doesn't extend to their personal assets (but there are important exceptions). Similarly, the stockholder "owners" are liable only to the extent of their investment in stock, should the corporation fail. This limited liability is why many businesses incorporate.

For small businesses, the main disadvantages of incorporating are the effort and cost. To incorporate, in part, you must:

• draft "bylaws,"

• submit "articles of incorporation" to the state agency which charters corporations,

• await approval and

• issue capital stock and record its subscription.

Unless you have time and ability to do this yourself, legal fees for incorporating can amount to several hundred dollars.

Once incorporated, there are ongoing requirements to:

• make some decisions only with the approval of directors or stockholders and record their approval, or "resolutions," in a "corporate minutes" book;

• conduct annual stockholders' meetings;

• elect directors and officers annually and

• file "annual reports" with the state.

It would appear that corporate profits, in contrast to those of a sole proprietorship or partnership, are taxed twice. First, as an entity, a corporation pays corporate income taxes on its profits. Then, a portion of remaining profits is distributed as dividends, on which stockholders must pay personal income taxes. Is incorporating not worth the hassles? Before you conclude that, you may want to discuss one type of corporation, the "S corporation," with your accountant and attorney.

"S Corporation"

The "S corporation," named for its section of corporate law, is like any other corporation in terms of legal requirements. Its difference is that its profits pass through to stockholders, proportionately to their share of the stock. In this sense, it's like a partnership. The S corporation files tax returns, but they're informational; there's no corporate income tax. The S corporation offers the small business person limited liability and possible tax advantages. Discuss with your accountant and attorney which legal form of business is right for you, at least initially. As your business grows, you can change your legal structure to one which meets your changing needs.

Other Legal Requirements

At this point, you've outlined the services you'll provide, decided who will help you and, with professional help, selected the legal structure your business will take. Let's say that taxes and limiting your liability are important to you, so you've elected to do business as an S corporation. Your attorney has drafted bylaws and submitted articles of incorporation for state approval. Aside from awaiting your charter, have you met all the legal requirements for beginning service? Not quite. Depending on where you "do business," (where your office is located <u>and</u> where you provide service) there are a few more things you must do.

First, you should select and register with the state your "ASSUMED BUSINESS NAME." An "assumed" or "fictitious" business name is one which does not fully name all owners. "Sadie A. Smith, Pet Sitter" does name the owner fully so needn't be registered as an assumed business name, unless there are other owners. "Sadie's Pet Sitters" is an assumed business name, because it doesn't fully name Sadie, and it implies there could be additional owners.

Registering your business name

You've probably already selected a name for your business, but this is a good time -- before registering it -- to be sure it's right for you. Consider if it's both functional and appealing to customers. Is it clear and descriptive? "Bill's Pet-Care-At-Home" describes the service; "Bill's TLC" doesn't. A play on words (e.g., "Paws for Awhile") can be appealing and memorable, but be careful yours isn't too nebulous.

Is your name the same as or strikingly similar to one already in use? The resulting problems are obvious. You or your attorney should contact the state to insure there's not a similar assumed business name already registered.

Next comes BUSINESS LICENSES. Contact all cities (and smaller communities having city halls) and counties where you will provide service, ask if business licenses are required and make application. When contacting the city in which you reside, ask if a home occupation permit is required if you intend to locate your office in your home.

Business licenses

States require certain kinds of business activity to apply for licenses or permits. Ordinarily, pet sitting is not included, but check with your state's commerce department to be sure you're exempt. The surest way to know you're meeting local, county and state requirements is to contact their offices or a Chamber of Commerce and obtain a checklist for starting a small business in your area.

In addition to these requirements of most businesses, yours may face a few others.

Federal ID number

If your business will be a partnership or a corporation (including S corporation), <u>or</u> if you will hire and pay employees, then it must apply to the IRS for a FEDERAL IDENTIFICATION NUMBER. This registers the business with the IRS, Social Security Administration and Department of Commerce.

Employees

"EMPLOYEES" -- this is a complex issue which we glossed over in discussing what help you'll need. This is a good time -- while considering legal requirements -- to give more thought to employees. For us, the decision, largely, has been financial.

Can you afford employees? Realize that your profits erode as salary, payroll expenses and overhead consume the service fees you collect. Here's where, "You get what you pay for," <u>really</u> rings true: don't think you can find, hire, train and keep a quality employee for minimum wage! Check around; determine how much fast-food restaurants in your area are paying, then how much pizza shops pay drivers with their own cars. You'll be surprised -- wages have risen sharply since we had summer jobs as kids! But your payroll costs will go far beyond wages; they'll include:

• FICA tax (Social Security),

• federal unemployment tax,

• state unemployment tax,

• workers' compensation insurance and perhaps

• local employment and/or transit taxes.

You'll also need to consider reimbursing employees for gasoline and the use of their own cars (wear and tear).

We said before that employees give you man-hours but require your man-hours to administer and supervise. To begin, can you locate and hire the "right" people -- employees you can train and trust to do what you expect (at a wage you can afford)? Can you motivate and supervise them to continue meeting your service standards? Will you have time to manage their problems and their payroll? Perhaps so, but give these issues long thought before you hire. And because the laws involving employees and taxes change frequently, you certainly should discuss employment with your accountant and attorney.

More an option than a requirement, you may want to consider PROTECTION for your business name and logo. Your name identifies your business, and so can an attractive, clever logo. Not every business uses a logo, but when used on fliers, brochures, business cards and stationery, it's an eye-catcher. You must decide if protecting your name and logo from use by others is worth the costs of registering them under state or federal law. Conducting a trade name or trademark search can be expensive. If you plan to do business only locally, then the protection may not be worth the cost.

Insurance

Obtaining appropriate business insurance may not be a legal requirement, but it certainly is important. Under legal structures of business, we discussed owners' liability. Insurance can protect business and owners' assets in the event that others claim damages or losses as a result of your business activities. This protection and the insurance which provides it are vital. Just as you "shopped around" for the right accountant and attorney, select an insurance agent or broker who is interested in working with you long-term. Describe your services and discuss your needs so that he can arrange an adequate GENERAL LIABILITY policy. General liability insurance applies to accidental damage and personal injury, but it does not cover theft. If you'll have employees, you'll need a SURETY or DISHONESTY BOND to protect the business in the

**Insurance
and bonding**

event they steal from clients. The amount of the bond should be adequate to cover potential theft.

The other insurance cost of having employees is WORKERS' COMPENSATION, required by the states of all businesses. Workers' compensation pays the medical expenses and lost wages of an employee who is injured or becomes ill on or as a result of his job. Dishonesty bonds and workers' compensation insurance can be expensive overhead costs; don't overlook them when considering whether or not to hire employees.

Using your car for business purposes, especially driving between pet sitting visits, can increase your AUTO INSURANCE costs. Discuss this with your insurance agent and ask him to shop for, perhaps, a better auto policy.

Setting Up Your Office

Enough bureaucracy for now! How about doing something that makes your business more tangible, gives it some dimension you can see? It's time to set up the office. Your office will be your business "shell" or "home base" where you collect tools (from paper supplies and service documents to accounting records) and organize and coordinate all business activities.

You need an office

You won't need a lot of space, but your OFFICE'S LOCATION is important. Although some professionals argue they can work out of a briefcase, the trunk of a car or off a kitchen table, we urge you to establish a more formal office. If it's to do its part keeping your business organized, then it must be an adequate facility.

Perhaps your first thought is to work out of your home, to avoid having to rent office space. There certainly are advantages, like accessibility. How convenient to merely walk across the hall to get to work -- think of the time and rent you'll save! But there are disadvantages, too. They involve the line which everyone must draw between his professional and personal lives. On one hand, working out of your home makes it difficult to "leave work." After hours, the office phone rings or you remember to do something, and suddenly, you're back at work. That lack of privacy may irritate your family. (If you're willing to draw the line, you can fix the problem with an answering machine and discipline.) On the other hand, a <u>non</u>-workaholic working out of his home fights the inclination to approach work a little more casually, "going in" late or when he feels like it. The fix, here, involves discipline, too. Either way, you've got to draw your line and maintain a schedule. Discipline yourself when to go to work and when to leave it.

Does your home provide an adequate area for your office? A spare bedroom may be perfect; a corner in the dining room doesn't give enough privacy or space.

A word of warning regarding rent and utilities: if you set up an office at home, talk to your accountant before you decide to "write off" a portion of your homeowner's expenses.

How should you EQUIP YOUR OFFICE? Begin with a table or desk, an appropriate chair and adequate lighting. Add a telephone. If your office is in your home, consider adding a separate business line for privacy and a professional image. If you're a corporation, check with your attorney: your state may require separate personal and business phones. If you add a telephone recorder or "voice-mail" type service, you can "take" phone calls around the clock (important if you want clients to advise you when they arrive home). Consider a service or recorder which has a remote retrieval feature so you can access your messages while making service calls. You'll require a typewriter for professional-looking service documents and correspondence. If you don't type, consider enrolling in a typing course at a local business school or community college.

Equipping your office

Your <u>filing system</u> is important, because it allows you to keep, organize and access your business records. Begin with a sturdy, locking file cabinet which has at least two drawers. We recommend you set up dividers for two sets of files, "General" and "Financial." Here's the filing system which we found works for us. Modify it to meet your particular needs:

• GENERAL (current year)

A filing system that works

-     Animals, General

-     Client Files (subdivided, alphabetically)

-     Competition

-     Correspondence

-     Employees, Prospective

-     Employment, General

-     Employment, Training

-     Forms, Client Service Agreement

-     Forms, Daily and Weekly

-     Forms, Employment

-     Forms, Training

-     Insurance

-     Legal

-     Licenses, Permits and Registrations

-     Marketing

-     Monthly Schedules, Completed

-     Monthly Schedules, Pending

-     Office Supplies (catalogs, information)

-     Pricing

- Printing

- Publicity

- Recommendations

- Service Agreements, Backup Copies

- Telephone Services

• FINANCIAL (current year)

- Accounting, General

- Accounts Payable

- Banking

- Daily Reports, Reconciled

- Expense Reports, Completed

- Expense Reports, Current

- Forms, Financial

- Hold for Payment

- Invoices Paid

- Ledger

- Loans

- Payroll

- Revenue

- Taxes

• Last year's General and Financial records.

We'll discuss forms and the contents of these files in Chapter 4, DAY-TO-DAY ORGANIZATION -- RUNNING THE BUSINESS.

Managing your files

A couple of important notes about your filing system:

• Since you could be liable for the misuse of client information which an intruder might find, be sure you keep files locked in their drawers when you're not in the office.

• If you happen to have a personal computer (or decide to buy one as your business grows), you'll want to consider software programs which can replace some of these paper files.

At the beginning of each year, "clean out" your filing system. Make up new General and Financial files. Retain last year's Financial files right behind this year's. Go through the General files and move anything pertinent (e.g., client files, valid insurance policies) to this year's new files. Leave dated contents in last year's General files, then move these and Financial files from year-before-last to a storage box. Locate the box where it's secure and fairly accessible.

Having more than two drawers in your cabinet allows you to store office supplies and bulk quantities of forms and marketing materials.

Next, you need a client and vendor "<u>data</u> <u>base</u>." For quick access to phone numbers and information, purchase an index card file and a large supply of lined 4 x 6 cards. We recommend that you use a standard format and type each card so you know where to look and can find information quickly. Locate the card file next to your telephone. Again, to protect your clients, don't show home security codes or other sensitive information on their cards.

Security of client keys

To reduce "non-revenue" time spent in picking up and returning keys, you'll urge repeat clients to entrust duplicate keys to you. This is easier for you and the client -- as long as you keep the keys in a safe location. Because of the security burden this places on you, an <u>adequate</u> <u>key</u> <u>repository</u> is very important. Since burglars can simply carry off a small safe, consider a non-mobile repository, hidden in or near your office. Never put clients' names on their keys.

Instead, develop your own coding system. Be sure to locate your decoding chart where you can find it, but where an intruder won't know what it is.

Purchase enough office supplies to get started: tablets, pencils, pens, a stapler, typing ribbons and paper, paper clips, scissors, file folders and labels, an "in" basket or vertical file holder for your desk, a desk calendar (we recommend a large pad) and a dictionary. To reduce office expenses, consider joining a club-like, wholesale office supply house, if there's one in your area.

Your office looks equipped, now, but you still have <u>mail</u> and <u>banking</u> to arrange. A P.O. box is a must.

"Why? Whatsa matter with getting mail at my street address?"

If you want to avoid the heartache of kittens or puppies left on your doorstep, don't use a street address in correspondence or marketing. And you don't want to encourage clients and others to drop in on you at the office. If your office is at home, your insurance may not cover others' accidents on the premises, and there could be local ordinances against, say, street parking. Another address consideration is the telephone directory -- be sure it doesn't list your street address.

A commercial checking account, separate from your own, is a must and a legal requirement if you're a corporation. Again, show a P.O. box, not a street address, on your business checks.

By golly, your office looks great! Aside from a few forms and marketing aids, you've got your tools together. Well, almost. How about TRANSPORTATION? That's going to be a big part of your pet sitting service.

Transportation

Gas, insurance and basic maintenance for your '63 bug may be cheap, but will the car meet your business needs? Is it safe? Can you count on it? What kind of shape is it in? If you've contracted to walk a dog, morning and evening, you've <u>got</u> to be there for him, unless he knows how to use a litter box or toilet. What will your transportation backup be if your car breaks down? Can you fix it, borrow a car? If your car is mechanically reliable, is it comfortable? You'll be in it for hours each day - does it have adequate back support and heat? Do you need air conditioning? It just may be time to think about getting a new or different car.

"All right - a new car!"

Can you "write off" your new car as a business expense? It can be done, but it's not simple. Consult your accountant. He'll probably urge you, instead, to take mileage-based reimbursement for the business use of your car.

Alright, that's it! You're ready for business, right?! The phone rings. It's your veterinarian. She's heard you're starting a pet sitting business, and she'd like to help.

"Tell me about your services and fees. Can you bring me some brochures?"

Whoops ... you're not ready yet!

3

Marketing

What is "Marketing?"

The problem, at this point, is that no one -- potential clients or those who can bring them to you -- knows about your new pet sitting business. "Getting the word out" involves "marketing." What is marketing? There probably are as many definitions as there are people involved in it. The definition we like is: those planning and promoting activities which sell a product or service.

If your marketing is effective, then demand for your services matches supply (your capacity to serve), and the result is a steady stream of revenue. If you're "off-base" with ineffective marketing, supply and demand end up out of balance, and revenue falls. One example is advertising over too broad a geographic area. It brings would-be clients from too far away so that you waste either gas and time serving them or telephone time turning them down. Similarly, advertising at the wrong time of the year brings business you can't serve. Christmas and spring break are heavy vacation periods when you can expect your regular clients to book you to capacity. If you advertise just prior to these times, you'll end up wasting more time turning down requests. And some may be from late-booking regular clients!

Advertising considerations

We've seen other examples of pet sitters' promotional errors. Doorknob pouches containing fliers may attract clients in a well-chosen neighborhood, but not in another. So will the response be weak if you leave fliers in the wrong shops, veterinarian offices and apartment complexes. Or if your literature over-emphasizes extra services which you can but prefer not to perform, then you might get many inquiries, say, just for yard work. Again, time wasted on the phone.

Effective marketing

What forms can marketing take? The spectrum is infinite, from word-of-mouth to media advertising, event sponsorships and airplane sky-writing. Forms which pet sitters commonly use are fliers or brochures, sales calls and local advertising. The challenge for you, with limited resources, is to think like a pet sitter (not a large national organization), then engage in effective marketing. How do you do that? By:

• reconsidering your services and who your clients will be,

• setting the right fees, then

• selecting the promotional means which sell your services best.

Refining Your Services

Earlier, under BASIC DECISIONS, we asked you to think about the services you'll offer. Now, as Vice President of Marketing, your first task is to re-examine those services and tailor them to your clients.

Tailor services to clients

Who will your clients be? Evaluate the "demographics" -- vital statistics or characteristics -- of people living in neighborhoods close enough to serve. Consider income. Given the choice between affluent and less affluent neighborhoods, shouldn't you concentrate your efforts on higher-income potential clients? They probably travel more, for pleasure and business. They're busy people who may not know many neighbors. And, they use many professional services.

But don't let apparent affluence -- big houses in new neigh-borhoods -- monopolize your attention. Some of those folks, burdened by huge mortgage and car payments, may not travel for years. Other demographic targets could be lucrative, too. Consider age: the folks who live in that nice neighborhood of older homes are retirees. In spite of their fixed incomes, many travel regularly. Some have pets, and others would, if they knew about your services.

Age

Consider professional status: that older-looking apartment complex may be filled with graduate engineers who just moved into the area to begin careers with the high-tech giant down the road. Many have pets, and business travel can be a problem for those who are single. They'd be eager for your services.

Professional status

"Wait a minute! Why all this 'demographic' stuff?! Why can't I just set a price, put my fliers in stores, then serve whomever calls me?"

You can, but remember your goal: <u>effective</u> marketing. You just identified two important components of success: price and stores, i.e., where people can find out about you. For your marketing to attract the right clients, you'd better consider their demographics in order to set prices correctly and know where to advertise. For example, if you live in a retirement community, be careful not to set your prices too high. Seniors probably have used fewer professional services through the years. Although they may be very interested, they'll regard your services as extravagant if priced too high for their fixed incomes. On the other hand, it's possible to set your prices too low for affluent clients. Willing to pay well for the professional services they use, they may ask, "How can she give me the service I require for that paltry fee?"

Stores, shops and offices -- people will pick up promotional literature if it's where they are and draws their attention. In distributing your materials, shouldn't you place them where they'll attract the clients you want? Look around at where they shop: delis, trendy markets, beauty salons, boutiques and specialty shops. It makes more sense to leave your fliers there than in supermarkets. Veterinarians' offices and pet supply stores are excellent flier locations, because patrons, there, are thinking about their pets. But there are a few traps to avoid: if a veterinarian serves a less affluent part of town, his clients may not travel or may not be able to afford

Distributing your literature

your services. Or they may live in the next community, too distant for you to serve. You'll waste either gas and time serving them or telephone time turning them down.

Demographics, then, help you decide which clients and areas to serve and where they are likely to pick up and read your promotional materials. And they require you to set realistic fees. How do you do that?

Pricing

PRICING is the first refinement to your services. It's a key to your success, and it's not quick and easy. Correct pricing is like a balancing act: there's the tendency to fall one way or the other, with prices too high or too low. How do you set your service fees at the right levels?

Earlier, when setting up your office, you shopped for an electric typewriter. You looked at three models priced at $199.95, $249.99 and $499.95. Obviously, their features were different, but did you wonder how the sticker prices were set?

A manufacturer takes two courses in setting his prices: a "cost approach" and a "market approach." In his cost approach, he adds up his design, material, production, marketing, distribution and overhead costs, then tacks on the profit which he expects (reasonable or otherwise) to see what price they suggest. Putting cost approach aside for a moment, he turns to a market approach -- what his customers are willing to pay. What can they afford? What do their spending habits show they're willing to pay for comparable products? After answering these questions, he recalls his cost analysis and compares its suggested price to what he thinks customers will be willing to pay. Hopefully, they're close enough to suggest one "sticker" price. If not, the seller will have to adjust by:

• reducing his costs,

• lowering his profit expectation, or

• accepting the risk that his price may be too high (although maybe he can compensate with strong salesmanship).

In the case of the $499.95 typewriter, the seller's cost approach may have suggested a price of $600, including a big profit. But his market approach found that customers buy comparable typewriters for $400-$500 and rarely are willing to pay more. To "move" his typewriters, he must sacrifice some of his profit expectation and lower his price.

"You mean I have to do both cost and market analyses to set my service fees?!"

Right. The pricing process is the same for a pet sitter as it is for a manufacturer or distributor: you have to consider your costs, profit expectation (realistic or modified) and what clients are willing to pay. It takes a little homework, but it's very important. Again, it's like a balancing act.

Your cost approach should ferret out all costs of your basic service call: professional fees, licenses, office supplies, rent and utilities (if you don't work out of your home), phone, insurance, marketing (printing, advertising), service supplies, automobile and payroll and employment costs, if you have employees. If your total costs add up, say, to $750 per month, and if your demographic studies suggest you'll average 5 visits per day, then your cost per visit equals $5:

$$\frac{\$750 \text{ total cost per month}}{30 \text{ days X 5 visits per day}} = \$5 \text{ cost per visit}$$

This is only an example; take time and be realistic in <u>your</u> cost approach.

Add your profit expectation to the cost per basic visit. What's reasonable? Consider what economists call your "opportunity cost" -- the value of your time, based on what you could be earning in another employment opportunity. If you have the training and could make $8 an hour as a clerk or $9-12 as an office manager, then $12 an hour is your opportunity cost and is a realistic profit expectation. Let's say you plan to spend an hour, including driving time, on each basic visit. Then, our examples suggest a cost approach price of $17 per visit ($5 cost plus $12 profit).

Opportunity cost

**What is the cost of
extra services?**

Before taking a market approach to pricing your basic service visit, cost out extra services you intend to offer. Simplest is to identify their "incremental" costs -- those you haven't already covered in the cost approach to pricing your basic service. Unless they involve tools or supplies, extra services just require more time. Time is easy to cost out. In the example above, opportunity cost values your time at $12 per hour. If you don't include dog walking or brushing pets in your basic service, and if you figure each will require (on an average) 15 minutes longer, then these extras cost out at $3:

$12 per hour opportunity cost X .25 hour = $3 incremental cost

Another "extra" might be serving clients who live beyond your service area. This is a little more complicated, because it involves not just time, but car expenses - gasoline and wear-and-tear. Here, you apply the mileage reimbursement which your accountant suggested you use, say 34¢ per mile.

"Do I have to figure driving distance to those clients' homes?"

Not exactly; it could get too complicated. Instead, draw circles, or service zones, on a map. Define them in distances from your office, based on driving conditions, average speed and time. As examples:

• "Zone 1," your "basic service" zone, might be a 0-7.5 mile radius from your office. You choose that distance, because you're willing to travel for 15 minutes to or from a visit, and you think average driving speed through the area is 30 miles per hour:

15 minutes X 30 miles per hour = 7.5 miles

There's no incremental cost within your basic service zone, because your time and transportation are included in the cost approach to your basic service fee.

- "Zone 2" might include outlying areas which are, say, 15 minutes (or 7.5 miles) further. Zone 2 incremental costs would be:

    opportunity cost = (15 min. + 15 min.) X $12 per hour = $6.00

    mileage = (7.5 miles + 7.5 miles) X 34¢ per mile   = 5.10

    incremental costs   = $11.10

- You could set up Zones 3, etc., but notice how your costs soar. Would clients accept fees high enough to cover incremental cost?

The market approach - what clients are willing to pay - deserves more consideration than many pet sitters give it. Perhaps you don't need it to predict that a "Zone 2" client in the example above would find your fees (based on costs) unaffordable, but it is necessary for setting fees at the right levels. In our experience, pet sitters tend to set fees too low. Don't assume that people in your area are willing to pay no more than, say, $10 per visit for a service new to them or for a new pet sitter.

Don't set your fees too low

The market approach involves a lot of checking around to predict what potential clients will pay. Ask people with pets. Determine what other pet sitters charge. Put yourself in your clients' shoes - what would you pay?

What people will pay involves "utility": the value, satisfaction or peace-of-mind a customer gets from a service or product. Find out how much utility your clients get, paying for weekly yard care. Maybe $20 worth? Now, how much utility do they associate with daily child care? By comparison, how much utility do your pet sitting services offer the client? The same as lawn care? No, far more! Same as child care? Many clients, loving their pets as they do, will say the utility is comparable. If that's the case and clients will pay, say, $10-20 per day for child care, then they're willing to pay the same for your services.

Utility

Okay, your market approach suggests a price range of $10-$20 for your basic services. But where in that range should you set your fee? You may want to do more utility analysis to narrow down the range. Talking to folks might reveal that, for pet sitting, they'd be willing to pay four times as much as for weekly indoor plant care, twice as much as for house cleaning or the same as for dinner out or catered two or three nights per week.

Cost approach vs. market approach

Now it's time to recall your cost approach and compare it to your market analysis. In the example, your cost approach suggested a $17 fee for a one-hour basic service visit (including driving time). Your market approach, pointing to a $10-20 price, confirms that $17 would be a realistic fee. But what if more utility analysis found that people really are willing to pay no more than $11-15 for pet sitting? Then, you'd have to either cut costs, lessen your profit expectation or take a chance that, at $17, you can convince clients that the service they'll get will be worth the higher price. Of these choices, your best bet might be to lessen your profit expectation. After all, there might not be any $12 per hour office jobs available to you at the moment. Or if available, they might be miserable. If you lessen your expectation to a more-realistic $10 per hour, then the resulting $15 cost figure fits into the $11-15 range suggested by the market approach.

Another way to reduce your costs per service call is to spend less time on each. We allocate an hour for each visit, on the average, because we feel time is an important ingredient of quality. You may not agree. If your opportunity cost is $10 per hour, and your other costs are $5 per visit, then cutting your service time from one hour to thirty minutes reduces your visit costs from $15 to $10. However, if your clients want more than "quickie" visits and will pay more than $10, you'll have to decide how to "package" your services:

• as a $15, one-hour visit which offers free features like brushing, a short walk and watering house plants, or

• as a $10, half-hour visit with additional charges for any extra services or time.

Our clients like the simpler pricing of the longer visit. So do we.

Even if you decide on longer service calls with several free features, you'll want to address and price extras, because you'll get requests. Extra animal care and extra driving to/from distant clients are probably the most common. Use the same cost and market approaches to price extras. There's one we haven't mentioned, yet, because we were saving it to illustrate how easy it is to underprice services. Pre- and post-service calls to meet pets and owners, complete service agreements, exchange the key and maybe pick up payments, require your time and have associated car expenses. The cost approach might price out a half-hour pre-service call at $10.10 (15 miles X 34¢ per mile, plus $5 of your time).

Your new client responds, "What?! Ten bucks to pick up my key?!"

Wanting to avoid hostility, as most of us do, you're tempted to "comp" pre- and post-service visits, charging nothing at all. However, if you do this, you're giving away services which cost you to perform. Instead, you should keep in mind that clients do get utility for these special visits, even though there's no pet service involved. We've wrestled with the pre-/post-service dilemma, and we've settled on a two-part solution which works for us:

• We charge a $3 flat fee for each pre- and post-service visit. But some last more than thirty minutes, and there's no way the $3 fee covers our costs, so ...

• We also charge a slightly higher fee for our basic service visits to subsidize pre- and post-service calls.

A final warning on pricing. If you err -- price too high or too low -- can you change your fees? Sure, but consider two problems:

Do it right the first time

• You'll have to reprint and replace any literature which shows your old price, and

• it may be difficult to reattract clients alienated by your original fees.

It's easier to do something right the first time. Use the cost and market approaches in setting your fees.

Now that you've set your fees, do you need to REFINE

A menu of services

YOUR SERVICES FURTHER?

Perhaps. While studying your service areas and potential clients, you may have made discoveries which suggest you reflect a little longer on the menu of services you intend to offer. For example, you may have found considerable demand for yard care, but no end to the school-age entrepreneurs who provide that service for fees far lower than your costs. You'd be foolish to promote yard care. Or -- to your surprise -- you may have found that a high percentage of pets in your service areas are birds, rodents or reptiles. You should consider mentioning these in your promotional aids, since their owners may seek, first, pet sitters who know about their special needs.

"Refining" your services doesn't require that you decide not to do some. In fact, you'll want to remain open-minded and consider performing any reasonable service for which there's a need. What is important is that you promote those services most in demand in your service areas. "Promotion" is a key word, because it brings clients to you. But it has costs. The challenge in marketing is to promote effectively.

Marketing Tools

Your next step as Director of Marketing (or was that "Vice President?") is to DEVELOP YOUR MARKETING TOOLS. What are they? Since you're not General Motors, national TV advertising probably is not one. Those that pet sitters commonly use are:

A graphic identity

• A "logo," or graphic design, used on other marketing aids to identify your business. It's your trademark, whether you register it or not. Your logo probably will depict pets and/or your other home services. To be attractive and memorable, it should be simple, descriptive and unique.

• Business cards are usually the cheapest printed advertising and the easiest to distribute. You can leave them, mail them or hand them out. And they're convenient to carry. Be sure always to have them in your wallet or purse -- you never know where or when you'll encounter a potential client. Keep a large supply in your office. As with your business checks, show your P.O. box on your cards, not a street address.

• Fliers and brochures. The difference between these aids is the number of pieces of paper they contain. Fliers usually are a single piece of paper, printed on one or both sides, then folded one or more times. Brochures are printed on multiple pieces of paper which are then stapled together. Because pet sitting and home services aren't complex, a flier usually accommodates all information you wish to print. If you make your fliers a common size (e.g., double-folded letter size or triple-folded legal size), they'll fit nicely into commercial stands or holders, available at office supply outlets. If you find commercial dispensers too expensive, consider making them from white or colorful poster card.

Telling the world about your service

• Signs for your car turn it into a moving billboard! Magnetic signs, custom made by graphic arts shops, allow you to display and remove your signs at will -- or move them to a different car. Effective signs easily capture the eye:

"SADIE'S PET-SITTING
222-CARE"

Signs are great, but be ready for one security aspect: some clients may not want your signs in their driveway, advertising that they're not home.

• Letterhead, notepads and other handouts, printed with your business name and logo, certainly promote your services. Are they worth their costs? That depends on how and where you use them.

"Hey, how come you haven't mentioned MEDIA ADVERTISING yet?!"

There's no question that advertising via newspaper, radio, TV -- and the phone directory -- can be an effective marketing tool, but it may have drawbacks for the pet sitter. First, it can be much more expensive than the aids discussed above, especially considering the short "life" of a one-time ad. Also, media advertising can be geographically too broad, attracting would-be clients who live too far away to serve. Two ways to counter the geography problem are to use "qualifiers" ("Serving the southwest neighborhoods") and use only local media vehicles, like neighborhood newspapers.

How do you develop your marketing tools? Put on your

"advertising hat!" Don't worry; you needn't be an accomplished writer or artist. Let's try it.

Developing your marketing tools

You've given a lot of thought to your services and the utility they'll provide. Try describing them in writing. Then rework the text, choosing better words. Now obtain the fliers of unrelated services and study how they're composed and laid out. On folded fliers, notice how the front panel identifies the business while interior panels describe its services and advantages. Next, fit your narrative into a similar format, but never copy anyone's promotional materials, especially another pet sitter's. Shorten and simplify your text to make it fit and to make it attractive and powerful. Eliminate words which are unnecessary and whole sentences which seem unimportant. Use "bullet points" or symbols to draw readers' eyes to major points:

"• Specializing in cat care"

After you've laid out your flier, leave it for a day. Then read and critique it. Do you still like it, or are there better ways to express the ideas? Finally, ask others to critique it.

There may be some information, like prices or certain services that you don't want to print in your flier. Why? Because they could change, and you don't want to reprint. Alternately, you could leave these subjects for phone discussion, or you can print or photocopy separate "stuffers", then insert these information sheets into your folded fliers. Stuffers are easier to change than fliers.

Developing the text of your flier as you did probably gave you some powerful short phrases or slogans which distinguish your services. You should consider using these gems as you design your business cards, signs and any other printed materials.

Let's discuss your logo. It should be unique, setting you apart from other pet sitters and businesses. Before you look at other logos (don't copy!), look around your home and develop your own ideas. Ours came from seeing a kitty sitting on a window sill, beside a potted geranium. Your logo should be simple, descriptive and appealing to the viewer's eye. It can be black-and-white, but consider adding a touch of color. If you're not satisfied with your artistic results, ask your printer -- or a graphic artist he recommends -- to help design an attractive logo for you.

In all your promotional material, written and graphic, be professional and "come from the heart." Keep your message simple and descriptive; allow no opportunity for confusion. Develop your own ideas; never plagiarize. If you use your own words, you'll remember them during sales calls and other opportunities.

Make sure it "comes from the heart"

Introductions

Speaking of sales calls, it's time to INTRODUCE YOUR NEW BUSINESS. Since you're anxious to begin service, you want to do this as fast, effectively and inexpensively as possible.

"How about the Yellow Pages?"

Again, consider cost and geographic coverage - does it correspond to your service areas? If not, then phone directory listings and advertising may not be your most effective introduction to the community. How about sales calls?

"Why sales calls? I don't know the first thing about selling techniques!"

The advantage of sales calls is that your prospective clients -- or those who can direct clients to you -- meet you face-to-face. They get to see first-hand what kind of person will perform the service. Advertising generally can't do that.

Selling has been described as an art and as a science. You can study selling strategy and techniques for years. Or you can boil it down and make it simple. In fact, if you believe in what you're selling and if you'll just be yourself, selling comes easily.

Your pet sitting services have utility, value! If you remember that and believe you're going to be the best pet sitter in town, then each sales call will get easier. What begins at 10:00 a.m. that first morning as:

> "Oh, excuse me sir, my name is John, and I'm starting a business, and would you mind if I just leave a few fliers and run ..."

will probably sound like this by 3:00 p.m.:

> "Good afternoon, Doctor! I couldn't help noticing how attractively you've arranged your brochures, here. Allow me to show you, please, how, with a simple addition -- no other changes -- we can make your display just a tad more appealing to your clients!"

This is exaggerated, but the point is, you'll gain confidence with experience. You'll discover selling techniques you didn't know you have.

Always be ready to "sell" your services

The first rule of sales is, "Know your product." Know your services, options, extras and prices. Be prepared to answer any question, quickly and confidently. A related rule is, always have an adequate supply of promotional aids when making sales calls -- business cards, fliers and dispensers. Pet sitters don't expect to "close a sale" when calling on, say, a pet store, but explain your services and advantages and leave your aids with proprietors so they can direct clients to you.

Who should you call on? It's possible to introduce yourself directly to clients (door-to-door, at group meetings), but effective marketing seeks to "get to" greater numbers of clients faster. Identify and call on those who can help you do this, those who are in contact with your would-be clients:

• veterinarians (even if they board animals, they know that some clients prefer home care),

- pet and supply stores,

- kennels (again, they may refer home care inquiries to you),

- travel agencies,

- realtors,

- corporate personnel departments (involved in relocating employees),

- trendy food stores and delis,

- salons and boutiques and

- apartments, condominiums and residence hotels.

The idea is to convince those who have regular contact with potential clients to promote your services for you. Why would they bother? Because your services (with all their utility) are a "goodwill product on their shelf." No one likes to say, "No, sorry; I have no idea how to help you." They'd rather say, "Yes, I have heard of a pet sitter! I've met her and, in fact, I have her brochure, here." That helpful service endears them to the client; it's to their advantage to refer you.

Help others sell you

At the same time you're making sales calls to introduce your business, start looking for mass exposure opportunities. Contact your newspaper's human interest editor -- if your services are new to him, he might be interested enough to write a feature article. Your TV or radio station also may consider featuring you in the consumer affairs section of a news broadcast. And civic groups, especially when introducing new members at regular meetings, offer you a chance to "network" -- meet new people and discuss your services.

Through sales calls, positioning your promotional aids, taking advantage of mass exposure opportunities and -- perhaps -- a phone directory listing and ad, you get the word out to clients that you're open for business!

Marketing Beyond Introductions

Word-of-mouth

There's another marketing tool we haven't mentioned, because we were saving it for now. As it is for us, it can be the core of your marketing program after you introduce your new business. The most effective marketing tool (get ready; here comes a pearl!) is WORD-OF-MOUTH. That is, if you have satisfied clients and others (veterinarians, shop proprietors) who hear you're the best, they'll do your promoting for you. When clients feel strongly about a service (good or bad), its reputation spreads geometrically, seemingly at the speed of sound. This is why quality service is so important. Can you think of marketing more effective than that which brings you all the clients you can serve, but involves almost no time or expense? We can't. Besides maintaining quality, the only support which word-of-mouth requires is adequate supplies of promotional aids and telephone time to service the many inquiries you'll get.

Even with effective marketing, your business will experience SLOW PERIODS. How do you deal with them? First, don't blame yourself; you're not doing anything wrong. Understand that "discretionary" travel (i.e., for pleasure) is cyclical, and business travel also has slow periods. Since pet sitting is related to travel, these business slumps pass through to you. Slow times often are predictable. Oregonians stay home during the beautiful early fall months. Arizonans prefer their own climate during winter and early spring, when residents of cold or wet states are evacuating to Hawaii, Florida and the Caribbean. To the extent you can anticipate slow periods, you can prepare and use the time wisely.

Slow times, first, are an opportunity to regroup after busy periods. If you've been working long hours without days off, it's time to catch up your personal affairs and consider a short vacation. Then, after returning, consider reinforcing your earlier marketing efforts. Repeat earlier sales calls, particularly on veterinarians and pet supply stores. Try to meet new people in those offices, but identify and call on the "decision makers" -- those most able to steer clients to you. Let them know you're successful (in case word-of-mouth hasn't reached them, yet) and ask permission to leave ample supplies of fliers, cards and dispensers.

If, after reinforcing earlier marketing, your bookings don't increase, then look for the problem's source. It's probably an economic trend or other conditions which are discouraging pleasure or business travel. Are there other marketing steps you can take to counter slow times? Sure:

Countering slow times

• Schedule and launch a sales "blitz" -- a wave of sales calls on additional shops, professionals and locations where new clients can find your fliers.

• Consider offering a small commission to travel agents who book your services for their clients. They're accustomed to receiving 7-15% commissions from airlines and other purveyors.

• This is a good time to consider certain discounts, such as to seniors or to clients who bring you new clients.

• Is this the time to place a newspaper, radio or TV ad? Perhaps, but consider cost and geographic coverage.

• Geography ... Perhaps this slow period suggests driving a little farther for new clients, at least for now.

"But if I discount, offer commissions and drive farther, I'm sacrificing my profits!"

Yes, a portion of your compensation. But at least you're covering the other costs of these new jobs and also carving away at overhead costs. These "marginal" jobs are worthwhile and bring you new clients. And you can restore your profit margin later, when economic conditions improve.

Quite the opposite of being willing to drive farther, you might consider working closer to home to reduce costs during slow periods.

"Right! How am I going to do that?! Is someone going to hand me a bunch of new clients?!"

Maybe. Ready for this? Consider working with your competitors! If you find you can work together, you might refer new inquiries -- or even clients -- to one another based on to whom they live closest. More on "friendly competitors" under Chapter 6, PITFALLS AND ADJUSTMENTS. Let's develop a few forms and procedures so you can start making service calls.

4

Day to day organization-running the business

Need for a "Routine"

You've seen by now that there's a lot more to pet sitting than just animal care. In fact, your service call is like the tip of an iceberg. Beneath it is your business -- all the planning, organizing and accounting which support service.

In Chapter 2, INITIAL ORGANIZATION -- GETTING STARTED, we introduce you to the legal and practical requirements of starting a new business. Now, we'll discuss the NEXT LEVEL OF ORGANIZATION -- the FORMS, PROCEDURES and REPORTS which allow you to start operating, then continue smoothly.

"Are you sure I need more paperwork?"

Yes. You need more organization.

Remember the reasons you're starting a pet sitting service -- profit motive, love of animals and the desire to run your own business. In other words, make some money while having a little fun. Unfortunately, "making money" is a dangerously-misunderstood phrase. Too many folks equate it with collecting revenue rather than realizing profit. We know there's a big difference between revenue and profit: costs. The only way to make money, i.e., realize profit, is to control revenue and costs.

You'll control revenue by putting your resources to best use -- marketing materials, advertising dollars and, especially, time.

Putting your resources to work

- "This is the wrong veterinarian to leave fliers with. He specializes in dogs, and I specialize in cats."

- "Why should I take a distant booking if I can make two or three visits here in my neighborhood in the same time?"

- "Mrs. Abernathy is Vice President of her company's new division. If I do an extra-special job for her, she'll recommend me to employees and maybe introduce me to the personnel manager."

Cost avoidance

The way to control costs is through "cost avoidance" decisions which are based on careful study of alternatives.

- "This seems too much to pay for printing fliers. I'll shop around till I find a better price."

- "That's just too far to drive for a two-week booking. With a little marketing, I can find clients closer to home and keep my car expenses down."

- "That's a terrific sale on personal computers! A PC could manage my client files, all records and bookkeeping! On the other hand, I spend less than an hour a day in the office. What little time I'd save wouldn't justify the expense, just now."

- "Letterhead printed with my logo would be nice, but with such light correspondence, now, I can do without it."

If you control revenue and costs, then you'll maximize your profit. How do you do this? The vehicle is a SIMPLE ACCOUNTING ROUTINE.

"Okay, stop! Hold it!! I'm not an accountant!"

And you don't need to be. We use "accounting" here, not in the sense of debits and credits, but to mean that you've got to be a little methodical and account for your activities, so you don't forget anything. "Routine" is the more-important word. It means you keep doing things the same way, so they become second nature.

There's no "best" routine. Take someone's, like ours, then modify it slightly to work for you. What's important is that yours contains sufficient prompts and checks so you don't overlook anything (e.g., a small expenditure, uncollected fees). Keep your routine simple and consistent, then use it! If you service and keep it neat, like a new car, it will continue serving and pleasing you.

"'Routine' is kind of a vague term. It's just a consistent way of doing things. What do you mean by a 'pet sitter's business routine?'"

Good question. Your routine will be the few forms, procedures and reports which guide you through planning, organizing and accounting for all your business activities. Your routine supports service by keeping track of what you're doing and controlling profit.

The first step in developing your routine is selecting your "vernacular" -- the words and phrases you'll use to describe your tools and activities.

"You're kidding! I have to give everything a name?"

Perhaps a customer doesn't care if you call him a "client," "booking," "job" or "visit." But you'll be calling on many people and doing a lot of speaking, promoting your services. The consistent use of professional-sounding phrases will dignify you as the professional you are. The vernacular you choose is entirely your choice -- develop it while you organize your business. Examples of our vernacular are:

Sound like a pro

• Since we offer service and encourage repeat bookings, we refer to each customer as our "client."

• Because we believe in personalized service, we don't make "calls" or "do jobs"; we make "visits."

• To us, forms and records which organize a plan (before events) are "schedules." Those which detail what actually happened (after events) are "reports." Remember this distinction as you study our routine; it'll help you read through it the first time.

Adopt these terms or choose your own vernacular. Just keep it simple, descriptive and appealing to others. Then use it, consistently!

Daily Routine

To begin developing your routine, let's imagine your first few hours in business. You're setting up files in the office when the phone rings. It's a prospective new client. You grab a pencil and tablet, since scribbled notes are the easiest way to capture information.

Your first booking

Mrs. Harris wants a little more information about you. Yes, she's seen your flier; she picked it up at her pet shop (you make a note which one, since it's obviously an effective marketing point). Otherwise, you'd offer to mail a flier. You probe with a few questions (while taking notes), give relevant information, "pitch" the advantages of your service and answer her questions. You did everything just right -- she wants to book your service.

Great, but not so fast. Before you accept the booking at your basic fee, make sure Mrs. Harris lives in your service area. A map on your office wall, showing zip codes or your service zones, helps you decide quickly if this booking would require extra driving. No problem. It looks like she lives 2-3 miles driving distance from the office. You want this booking, so turn to "light" conversation which gives you a wealth of information about Mrs. Harris, her pets, veterinarian, travel plans and how to find her house. You conclude by agreeing on a time to get together for final arrangements (or at least talk again) and by thanking her, warmly, for the booking.

Your first booking! But managing it requires some kind of RESERVATIONS SYSTEM.

"Why?"

So that, for any date, you know how many visits you're committed to, how many more you can book and you don't forget any. Our reservations system loosely parallels that of an airline, in that it features:

- inventory control,

- client data and

- booking detail.

A reservations system

Let's say you adopt our system. To examine its parts, let's see how you'll administer Mrs. Harris' booking.

Your large deskpad calendar gives you inventory control. To book Mrs. Harris' service, you write her name in the square of each date you'll visit her home and pets.

Fig. 1- Deskpad Calendar

Unless you plan the same capacity for every day, you may want to draw lines or write numbers in each square to show how many visits you think you can accommodate on that date. Each time a new client phones for service, you glance at your desk pad calendar to determine if you're still available for service on those dates. Your calendar is a changing inventory record - with successive phone calls, you'll commit service capacity or line out (or erase) cancellations. At the end of each month, remove that sheet from the calendar, fold it neatly, then file it with "Monthly Schedules, Completed."

The client card file

You transfer client data to (and store it permanently in) a 4 x 6 card file. We house ours in a plastic box beside the desk phone. During your phone conversation with Mrs. Harris, you took many notes. Now, let's transfer that information to a permanent record. Using a consistent format (so all cards show certain data in the same area, for quick location), type a card for Mrs. Harris.

File it alphabetically in the card file. Besides client cards, we also type cards for suppliers and all business and marketing

```
Name: ____ HARRIS, Jeanne & Lorren ____     Pets: Name, M / F, Age, Type
Address: __ 17937 Krasnoyarsk Place __      1. _Buffy (M) 6 Cocker Spaniel_
Apt. _____ Space M135 _____
City_ Portland _ State _OR_ Zip_97201_      2. _Beau (F) 9 Basset_____

Phone:___333-4094_____          3. _____

Referred By: _"Valley View" feature article_____
Vet is : _Dr. Wentworth_____ At: _West Valley Animal Clinic_____
Phone: __456-7891_____
Pet Medication: _Buffy (see Service Agreement)_____

Directions: _Central Ave. West to Milepost 14 (right side). Take first
  right (Pomona St). Third left is Krasnoyarsk. Trailer park at end
  of Krasnoyarsk. Go through entrance. M is 6th cul-de-sac on left.___

Contacts: ____Judy Wilson (Jeanne's sister) 234-5678_____
```

Fig. 2- 4 x 6 Client Card

contacts. Sometimes, a party can be two or more, so we file all cards together in the same box.

We maintain a formal client data file for the same reasons an airline or large hotel does:

• It saves a lot of questions and time when the client calls to book more service.

• It provides a handy name list for communicating service changes or mailing Christmas cards or promotional materials.

• Ready access to client information allows you to impress them when they call. "Of course I remember you, Mrs. Franklin! How are Spot and Fluff?" (But look at the next card to be sure you don't have two Franklins!) Typing cards in a standard format directs your eye to, say, pet names, quickly.

Your deskpad calendar only monitors inventory and capacity. To record the details of each booking, we need two more documents, a Monthly Schedule and a Service Agreement.

To create a Monthly Schedule, staple together three sheets from a 12-column accounting pad. Write the month and year at the top of the first sheet. Now identify the columns with successive dates. The purpose of your Monthly Schedule is to record important booking details which you'll need to organize each day's service. For each client, it will show:

The Monthly Schedule

• total number of visits,

• dates of first and last (circled in red) visits,

• special instructions or notes,

• total fee,

• whether or not you have the completed Service Agreement ("SA"),

• whether you have the client's key ("K") and

• if the client has paid the fee, yet ("Pd").

FEB 99 P.1   Monthly Schedule

No. of Visits SA?	Name	Fee Pd?	WED 01	THU 02	FRI 03	SAT 04	SUN 05	MON 06	THU 07	WED 08	THU 09	FRI 10	SAT 11	SUN 12
21 SA	Harris (pill Buffy daily)	$258	0	2	3	4	5	6	7	8	9	10	11	12
5 SK	Cortez	66	0 p.m./mail	2	3	4	(5) arrange post-six							
7 SA	Abraham	108	(1) H. D/bkyrd	2	BH.Offil yd	4	BH.D.bky.6		(7) H.Ofit					
1 SA	Brown	12 Pd	0											

FEB 99 P.1

	No. of Visits SA?	Name	Fee Pd?	WED 01	THU 02
K?					
K	21 SA	Harris (pill Buffy daily)	$258	0	2
K	5 SK	Cortez	66	0 p.m./mail	2
K	7 SA	Abraham	108	(1)H.D/bkyrd.	2
K	1 SA	Brown	12 Pd	0	

Fig. 3- Monthly Schedule

Notice that each date shows the number of each client's visit (i.e., his 7th, 8th, etc.). This and the total number of visits tell you at a glance (especially when a booking extends into the next month) how you're progressing through each commitment.

To position Monthly Schedules for convenient daily use, fold them neatly to letter size, then file them in "Monthly Schedules,

Pending" (sequenced with current month in front). At the end of each month (since you've already performed the service), transfer that Monthly Schedule from "Monthly Schedules, Pending" to "Hold for Payment." It will remain there until you show "Pd" beside each booking.

"Recording each booking twice seems like double work. Why do I have to do that?"

Because your deskpad calendar and Monthly Schedule have very different purposes:

• The calendar shows -- with a one-second glance -- who is booked and if you can perform more service on given dates.

• Monthly Schedules detail information you'll need to organize each day's service visits.

Neither record can perform the other's function. We said the Monthly Schedule records booking details. That's half-correct. It gives enough information about each booking to organize a day's service routine, but not enough to perform a visit. For example, Mrs. Harris' entry on the Monthly Schedule doesn't tell you:

• which of the two dogs is Buffy or when to give him how many pills, or

• just how to find 17937 Krasnoyarsk Place, Space M135.

Following your phone conversation, you may have typed some of this information onto Mrs. Harris' client card, but to get the level of detail you'll need in order to perform her service, you'll need to complete a Service Agreement. You can fill in some of it in the office, but to complete it, you'll need Mrs. Harris' help and signature. Earlier, you concluded your phone conversation with her by agreeing to get together to firm up details. During this pre-service visit, you'll meet one another and her pets, discuss detailed instructions, get her house key and complete the Service Agreement.

The Service Agreement

Service Agreement

Name: HARRIS, Jeanne   Directions to Home: Central Ave. to
Address: 17937 Krasnoyarsk Place   MP14, 1st Rt. Pamona. Third
             Space M135   light Krasnoyarsk, Ent. "M" 6th
City: Portland   State OR Zip 97201   st. on left, 3rd Sp. Lt = M135.

Home Phone: 333-4094   Office Phone: NA   Ext. NA

Name(s) and Description(s) of pet(s):
1.   Buffy (M) 6 Cocker Spaniel
2.   Beau (F) 9 Basset (jumps up!)
3.
4.
5.

Date Leaving   2/01/99   Time   9 AM   Date Returning   2/21/99   Time 10 PM

You can be reached at: 206/123-4567   Phone

Local Emergency Contact: Name   Judy Wilson   Phone   234-5678
                                (sister)
Persons with access to your home: only Judy Wilson

Your Vet: Name   Dr. Wentworth (West Valley)   Phone   456-7891

Other services included in our fees: ☒ Mail   ☒ Paper   ☒ Alter lights
                                         ☒ Water plants In yes   out fuschsia
                                         ☐ Other   (front door)

Special instructions: Buffy - pills on kitchen counter. Add
                          contents of 2 capsules to his fresh food each day.

Recycle cans?   ☒ Yes ☐ No

Location of food: Kibble in broom closet; meat in fridge.

(Company Name)   agrees to provide services from   Feb. 1   through   Feb. 21   .
Total number of visits   21   at $ 12.00   each, key pickup $ 3.00 , key return $3.00 ,
for a total of $ 258.00 . Services will be performed in accordance with the instructions
contained herein. The client waives any claims against (Company Name) unless (Company name)
is negligent and does not perform as agreed herein. Payment due upon completion. Please use the
attached envelope to mail payment on the date of your return.

_____   _Jeanne Harris_____
For (Company Name)   Client
Date: January 25, 1999   Date: January 25, 1999

Fig. 4- Service Agreement for Mrs. Harris

The Service Agreement is a key document:

• It's a contract between you and the client, specifying each party's responsibility (yours to perform service, Mrs. Harris' to pay you).

• It lists the client's emergency information -- phone contacts while away, others with access to her home, who her veterinarian is.

• It describes her pets, their idiosyncrasies and special needs.

• It details special instructions or extra services you've agreed to perform.

We recommend that, after you compose your Service Agreement and your attorney approves its wording, you have it printed as a three-part document:

• A white, top "working" copy for your use during service;

• A yellow, second copy for the client and

• A pink, third copy for an emergency or "backup" office copy, just in case you misplace the working copy.

Filing service agreements

After she signs the Service Agreement and you give Mrs. Harris her copy, bring the white and pink copies back to the office. File the working copy in "Monthly Schedules, Pending" and the backup copy in "Service Agreements, Backup Copies."

Returning from your pre-service visit, you also brought Mrs. Harris' key to the office. In discussing your office, we asked you to establish a secure repository for clients' keys. Keys are a big responsibility, because they represent access to your clients' homes. They trust that you'll keep their keys and homes secure while they're gone. To control keys, you must:

• identify each with a symbol (not a name!);

• locate an encoding/decoding chart where you can find it, but an intruder can't and

• ensure that an intruder can't access or remove your key repository.

Look around your office area and use your imagination -- it isn't too difficult to design an original repository.

Now it's the afternoon before your first service visit to Mrs. Harris' home. Since her booking, you've accepted a few more. In fact, your deskpad calendar shows four service visits tomorrow, and you also have a few business chores -- stops at the post office, bank, printer and an office supply store. To do all this efficiently (i.e., minimizing time and car expense), you'll need to organize tomorrow's daily service routine.

"Now don't tell me I need another form! I'll just start early, say 7:00 a.m., pick off the service visits, run the errands, then be back in the office by noon!"

Wrong. Look more closely at tomorrow's date on your Monthly Schedule. The Cortez visit shows "late p.m." You don't remember why, but the Service Agreement shows the client expects a large check in tomorrow's mail. He wants you to bring in the mail rather than let it remain in the mailbox overnight. The Monthly Schedule also shows tomorrow is the day you'll water Mr. Abraham's entire back yard for extra fee. You won't be back by noon!

The Daily Schedule

What you need for organizing your service routine each day is a Daily Schedule.

("Groan!")

It's not a chore -- write it out longhand on a tablet sheet. Do it each afternoon, so you have time to detect and correct problems, like not having a client's key, yet. At the top of the sheet, list the day and date, like "WED 2/01." Take your booking details (i.e., your current Monthly Schedule and working copies of Service Agreements) from "Monthly Schedules, Pending", then study what you have to do tomorrow. Look at a map, if necessary, and decide on the most efficient route. Be careful, again, that your itinerary honors special commitments ("a.m.," "p.m.") noted on the Monthly Schedule and explained in that client's Service Agreement.

Daily Schedule

WED 2/01

X K 1. Abraham — water back yard + blueberries.

X K (2.) Brown — home tommorow: leave note + pay envelope.

X K 3. Harris — pills for Buffy, water fuchsia.

X K 4. Cortez — after 3⁰⁰ᴾ: check in mail.

- bank

- post office - postage

- FasPrint - new Svc Agreements
      - fliers
- Ace Office Supply - ledger
         - 6 column pads
         - money rcpt books (2)

Fig. 5- Daily Schedule

Remembering that you're now responsible for the well-being of several living creatures, do a check and double-check to insure you're not overlooking a visit. First, look at the visits which the Monthly Schedule shows for tomorrow. Place a check (✓)in front of every corresponding entry on the Daily Schedule you've just written. Did you show all visits? Check one more time - look at your deskpad calendar and tomorrow's date square. Now cross-check (\) corresponding entries on the Daily Schedule. As long as you dutifully recorded all bookings on your calendar and Monthly Schedule, you can be sure you've not overlooked anyone for tomorrow.

Check and crosscheck

Your Daily Schedule is almost complete. Look at the Monthly Schedule, again, and see if it shows any last-day red circles or special instructions notes. If so, transfer these to your Daily Schedule. Naturally, you'll do a perfect job during every visit but, to promote your reputation for quality service, you might look for opportunities to do "little extras" during last-day visits.

**Assembling your
Service Kit**

The next step in organizing tomorrow's service routine is assembling a Service Kit. Use an inexpensive vinyl tablet holder which has pockets inside both covers, a small pocket for business cards and a flap or clip for a pen. Inside the right pocket, place a 12-month calendar (comes in handy during discussions at pre-service meetings) and the tablet on which you've made your Daily Schedule. In the left pocket, insert:

• a supply of extra fliers,

• all working copies of tomorrow's Service Agreements, and

• a supply of stamped, self-addressed envelopes to leave with
  clients for mailing you their payment.

Now add business cards and a pen. If your Service Kit won't accommodate a spare pen, put two or three in your car. Add a large, stiff paperclip on the left pocket. You'll use this to transport your banking - checks, deposit tickets and deposit receipts.

You are now ready for tomorrow's service visits and business chores.

Before "hitting the road," you'll need clients' keys and -- one more document -- a Daily Report, to record what you actually do. As you place today's keys on your keychain (more about that in the next chapter), mark a red "K" beside clients' names on your Daily Schedule. Don't leave till you see that you have all the keys you'll need.

Your Daily Report

Your Daily Report is merely a sheet from a 6-column accounting pad. Place it on a clipboard so you can make entries, easily, in your car.

As you make service visits and do business chores, record on your Daily Report:

• today's date and the time you arrive at each location,

• name and address,

• beginning, ending and resulting mileage,

- purpose (e.g., "service", "pre-service", "banking", "office supplies") and

- revenue earned as a result of a visit.

FEB 99
pg. 1
Daily Report

Date	Time	Name	Address			Beginning	End	T/M	Purp.	Rev.	#
2/01	1100	Abraham	2105 SW 67 Ter			31194	-97	3	Svc	18	
	1245	Brown	8817 SW 90 Ave				-99	2	"	12	
	1341	Harris	17937 Krasnoyarsk Pl				-03	4	"	12	
	1455	Cortez	8540 Williamsburg Way				-04	1	"	12	
	1550	2nd Nat'l Bank	3636 SW Main				-08	4	banking	—	
	1610	Post Office	4027 SW 72 St				-11	3	mail	—	
	1625	FasPrint	1122 Broadway, Bty				-14	3	printing	—	
	1642	Ace Office Supply	8910 Broadway, Btn				-15	1	supplies	—	
	1650	home					-18	3	—	—	
02	0930	Abraham	2105 SW 67 Ter			31221	-24	3	Svc	12	
	1020	Harris	17937 Krasnoyarsk Pl				-28	4	"	12	
	1125	Cortez	8540 Williamsburg Way				-29	1	"	12	
	1220	2nd Nat'l Bank	3636 SW Main				-33	4	dep	—	
	1230	Post Office	4027 SW 72 St				-36	3	mail	—	
	1255	home					-39	3	—	—	
03	1000	Abraham	2105 SW 67 Ter			31245	-48	3	Svc	18	
	1130	Harris	17937 Krasnoyarsk Pl				-52	4	"	12	
	1225	Cortez	8540 Williamsburg Way				-53	1	"	12	
	1330	Western Pet	7204 SW Harris				-56	3	supplies	—	
	1405	home					-59	3	—	—	
	1510	Post Office	4027 SW 72 St				-62	3	mail	—	
	1520	home					-65	3	—	—	
04	1015	Abraham	2105 SW 67 Ter			31270	-73	3	Svc	12	
	1120	Harris	17937 Krasnoyarsk Pl				-77	4	"	12	
	1230	Cortez	8540 Williamsburg Way				-78	1	"	12	
	1325	Post Office	4027 SW 72 St				-81	3	mail	—	
	1342	home					-84	3	—	—	
05	0930	Abraham	2105 SW 67 Ter			31289	-92	3	Svc	18	

Fig. 6- Daily Report

If today will be busy or you're getting towards the end of a Daily Report, attach a second, blank sheet to the clipboard.

Daily Report information is necessary:

• to complete your Expense Report, later, for reimbursement for use of your car,

• to monitor and reconcile collection of fees, and

• for payroll, if you hire employees to make service visits.

If you have employees, you'll probably need to revise your Daily Report to convert it to a payroll document. On the next page is a Time Sheet which might work for you.

Ask your attorney if this meets your state's current payroll requirements.

When your entries bring you to the end of a Daily Report sheet, carry over to a fresh sheet. Place the filled-out Daily Report behind the new one, return it to the office and file in "Hold for Payment."

Make the reports a habit

Each time you arrive at your next destination, take a minute to make the Daily Report entries. It's easy to forget, so force yourself to develop the habit. Make it second nature, so you make entries without thinking about them.

Your daily service routine is the subject of the next chapter. Let's skip over it for now and continue with forms, reports and procedures - the organizational routine which supports service.

Once back in the office, it's time to "regroup" - check that you've completed all service, finish recording what you did, service the phone and mail and organize tomorrow's Daily Schedule. First, check your Daily Schedule and verify you made all visits. Seeing that you did, return clients' keys to the repository. Next, calculate from your Daily Report how many miles you drove today, then record that in today's column of your Expense Report. Here's the Expense Report we use.

Time Sheet – Barbara

Date	Times			Name	Address		Mileage			Purpose	Rcv
	Dep. for/Ar. at	Pay ST	OT				Beginning	Ending	TM		
3/05	1120 1130	:30		Anderson	13927 NW View Ter		24120	-25	5	Svc	12
	1150 1200	1:00		Montoya	15201 NW Ridgeway Ct			-28	3	"	12
	1250 1300	:40		Ryan	14717 NW Lynnwood			-31	3	"	12
	1330 1345	:30		Zakress	1950 River's Edge Way			-36	5	"	12
	1400 1415	1:20		Klaus	3715 Goble St			-38	2	"	12
	1520 1530	:10		home				-42	4	—	—
Sub:		4:10							22		
3/06	1055 1115	1:00		Anderson	13927 NW View Ter		24152	-57	5	Svc	12
	1155 1205	:30		Montoya	15201 NW Ridgeway Ct			-60	3	"	12
	1225 1235	:50		Ryan	14717 NW Lynnwood			-63	3	"	12
	1315 1325	:35		Zakress	1950 River's Edge Way			-68	5	"	12
	1350 —			(personal)						—	—
	1455 1450	:50		Klaus	3715 Goble St		24175	-77	2	Svc	12
	1525 1535	:10		home				-81	4	—	—
Sub:		3:55							22		
3/07	1025										

Wk Totals **21:15** (signature of Pet Sitter) **114**

Fig. 7- Time Sheet

Employee Expense Report

Week of 2/01/99

To Whom Paid	Reason For Expenditure	Acct	2/01	2/02	2/03	2/04	2/05	2/06	2/07	Totals
USPS	postage	09	25.00							25.00
Western Pet	pooper scooper, etc.	14			11.96					11.96
Valley Food	welcome-home fruit	13						4.15		4.15
									(118)✓ (12)	
Mileage @ .325		02	(24) 7.80	(18) 5.85	(20) 6.50	(14) 4.55	(14) 4.55	(16) 5.20	3.90	38.35
Daily Totals			32.80	5.85	18.46	4.55	4.55	9.35	3.90	79.46

Employee Signature	Date 2/07/99	Total Expenses on this report	79.46
Job Title *President*		Add Previous balance due employee	-0-
Supervisor's Signature	Date 2/07/99	New Balance due employee	79.46
Job Title *Secretary*		Check # 106 Issued 2/07/99	79.46
		Carry forward balance due employee	-0-

Fig. 8- Expense Report

Expenses

To calculate your reimbursable mileage expense, multiply miles by the reimbursement rate which your accountant suggests you use. During 1998, for example, we "claimed" and showed as a legitimate business expense reimbursement at the IRS-allowed rate of 32-1/2 ¢ per mile.

You'll also want to show on your Expense Report any out-of-pocket legitimate business expenses. Examples would be the cost of postage stamps, office supplies or service supplies for which clients will reimburse you, later. Record these expenses, then attach their receipts to the back of your Expense Report.

If today's activities and entries complete your current Expense Report, then you or the Comptroller (also you ...) can close it out by issuing an expense reimbursement check. Record the check number on the Expense Report, file it in "Expense Reports, Completed," then hold the check copy for posting to the books in a few minutes. If you have employees, you'll probably require them to submit their Expense Reports and Time Sheets for approval and processing on a given day each week. If today's entries don't complete your Expense Report, file it in "Expense Report, Current."

Before turning to daily bookkeeping, let's clean out and prepare your Service Kit for tomorrow.

Getting ready for tomorrow

After verifying -- one more time -- that you've completed today's service, discard your Daily Schedule. It has served its purpose. If you chose to put off a chore, like buying office supplies, carry that over to tomorrow's Daily Schedule (make a note in the margin; you can sequence the stop later). Since most of your bookings are for several days, leave those Service Agreement working copies in the left pocket. For those bookings which today's service completed, remove their Service Agreements and file them in "Hold for Payment." Now, since you've completed those bookings and their working copies are secured back in the office, you can remove corresponding backup copies from "Service Agreements, Backup Copies" and <u>destroy</u> them. To protect customer information, don't simply discard them.

Since today was your first service day, you probably collected no fees. When you do, however, be thorough and quick in handling them:

• Bring payments back to the office, paperclipped inside your Service Kit.

• Stamp checks for deposit. List payments on a bank deposit ticket.

• Place cash, checks and their bank deposit ticket in an envelope, then paperclip that back into the Service Kit for tomorrow's deposit.

• Record the receipt of payment in a book of two-part money receipts.

DATE _2/02/99_ 19 ___ NO. _2701_

RECEIVED OF _Judy Brown_

ADDRESS _9817 SW 90th Ave_

Portland, OR 97219 $ _12.00_

FOR _1 visit @ 12.00_

HOW PAID _CK_

BALANCE DUE _-0-_ BY _____

DATE _2/07/99_ 19 ___ NO. _2702_

RECEIVED OF _Tony Cortez_

ADDRESS _8540 Williamsburg Way_

Portland, OR 97219 $ _66.00_

FOR _pre+post @ 3.00 + 5 visits @ 12.00_

HOW PAID _CK_

BALANCE DUE _-0-_ BY _____

DATE _2/09/99_ 19 ___ NO. _2703_

RECEIVED OF _Jay Abraham_

ADDRESS _2105 SW 67th Ter_

Portland, OR 97201 $ _108.00_

FOR _3 visits @ 12.00 + 4 visits @ 18.00 (watering)_

HOW PAID _CK_

BALANCE DUE _-0-_ BY _____

DATE _2/23/99_ 19 ___ NO. _2704_

RECEIVED OF _Jeanne Harris_

ADDRESS _17937 Krasnoyarsk Pl_

Portland, OR 97201 $ _258.00_

FOR _pre+post @ 3.00 + 21 visits @ 12.00_

HOW PAID _CK_

BALANCE DUE _-0-_ BY _____

Fig. 9- Money Receipt Book

On the money receipt for each payment, record the date of receipt, client's name, address, form of payment, number of visits, rate and total payment. Remove the top copy from the book and mail it to the client as his receipt of payment. Money receipt books, both current and completed, are filed in "Revenue."

Money receipts

"Why go through the fee calculation on the money receipt? The client doesn't care!"

Maybe he does. More importantly, you do, because the money receipt book is your permanent record of revenue received. You'll use it to reconcile revenue and to resolve your bookkeeping errors.

Reconciling revenue is necessary to ensure you collect what you earned. Discrepancies will occur as clients accidentally over- or under-pay you. It's also possible that you'll make extra service visits, with reason or accidentally. You'll want to identify these differences and resolve them with clients.

Reconciling revenue

To reconcile a client's payment, keep your money receipt book handy, then grab your "Hold for Payment" file. It contains Service Agreements, filled-out Monthly Schedules and filled-out Daily Reports.

"Don't say 'filled-out'; you mean 'completed.'"

No, that's the point -- these documents are awaiting payment entries, so they're not "completed," yet. But with the money receipt you just filled out, you can update or complete them now:

• Remove the Service Agreement, draw a diagonal line through it and mark it "Paid." File it alphabetically in your "Client Files," with the client's most recent Service Agreement in the front.

• Mark "Pd" in the client's line of the Monthly Schedule, then return it to "Hold for Payment." When all client lines show "Pd," then the Monthly Schedule is complete, and it can be moved to "Monthly Schedules, Completed."

If a client pre-pays you or pays for service shown on a current Monthly Schedule, then you'll find this in and return it to "Monthly Schedules, Pending" after noting payment.

Let's say you noticed a difference between the client's check (money deposit) and the total fee showing on the Monthly Schedule – the customer seems to have overpaid you by $12. Here's where the reconciliation occurs:

Locating discrepancies

• Take the filled-out Daily Report sheets from "Hold for Payment" (and maybe the current sheet on your clipboard), then locate the client's service dates. If you can't spot them quickly, the Monthly Schedule(s) will give you service dates. Mark a numbered check ($^1✔\,^2✔\,^3✔$ etc.) beside the revenue figure of each visit to that client's home (see Fig. 10).

Now compare the number of checks and fee entries to the number of visits and rate shown on the money receipt. If they don't match, you've located the discrepancy.

In the example of the $12 overpayment, you find an extra visit on your Daily Report. The prior day was to have been your last visit, but your deskpad calendar shows the client called from Hawaii and asked for one more day of service. You forgot to mark this on the Service Agreement and Monthly Schedule. Had the client paid the original fee, then your revenue reconciliation and the extra visit appearing on the Daily Report would have identified that discrepancy, too.

Following revenue reconciliation, return the money receipt book to "Revenue" and the Daily Report to "Hold for Payment." When all revenue entries have been checked off, the Daily Report is complete and should be moved to "Daily Reports, Reconciled."

Posting deposits

On those days you make bank deposits, clip the deposit receipts inside your Service Kit and return them to the office. Complete the deposit receipt by recording on the back (from corresponding money receipts) what the deposit represents:

"Why duplicate what I've already written into the money receipt book?"

You need this information to correctly post the deposit to

FEB 99
pg. 1

Daily Report

Date	Time	Name	Address			Beginning	End	TH	Purp.	Rev.	#
2/01	1100	Abraham	2105 SW 67 Ter			31194-	97	3	Svc	18	√/⓪
	1245	Broxon	8917 SW 90 Ave				99	2	"	12	√/1
	1341	Harris	17937 Krasnoyarsk Pl				03	4	"	12	√/1
	1455	Cortez	8540 Williamsburg Way				04	1	"	12	√
	1540	2nd Nat'l Bank	3636 SW Main				08	4	banking	—	
	1610	Post Office	4027 SW 72 St				11	3	mail	—	
	1625	FasPrint	N122 Broadway, Bytn				14	3	printing		
	1642	Ace Office Supply	8910 Broadway, Bytn				15	1	supplies		
	1650	home	—				18	3	—	—	
02	0930	Abraham	2105 SW 67 Ter			31221-	24	3	Svc	12	√/2
	1020	Harris	17937 Krasnoyarsk Pl				28	4	"	12	√/2
	1125	Cortez	8540 Williamsburg Way				29	1	"	12	√/2
	1220	2nd Nat'l Bank	3636 SW Main				33	4	dpos	—	
	1230	Post Office	4027 SW 72 St				36	3	mail	—	
	1255	home	—				39	3	—	—	
03	1000	Abraham	2105 SW 67 Ter			31245-	48	3	Svc	18	√/3
	1130	Harris	17937 Krasnoyarsk Pl				52	4	"	12	√/3
	1225	Cortez	8540 Williamsburg Way				53	1	"	12	√/3
	1330	Western Pet	7304 SW Harris				56	3	supplies	—	
	1405	home	—				59	3	—	—	
	1510	Post Office	4027 SW 72 St				62	3	mail	—	
	1520	home	—				65	3	—	—	
04	1015	Abraham	2105 SW 67 Ter			31270-	73	3	Svc	12	√/4
	1120	Harris	17937 Krasnoyarsk Pl				77	4	"	12	√/4
	1230	Cortez	8540 Williamsburg Way				78	1	"	12	√/4
	1325	Post Office	4027 SW 72 St				81	3	mail	—	
	1342	home	—				84	3	—	—	
05	0930	Abraham	2105 SW 67 Ter			31289-	92	3	Svc	18	√/5
	1040	Harris	17937 Krasnoyarsk Pl				96	4	"	12	√/5
	1135	Cortez	8540 Williamsburg Way				97	1	"	12	√/5
	1240	Post Office	4027 SW 72 St				00	3	mail	—	√
	1300	home	—				03	3	—	—	
06	0930	Valley Food	8240 Holbrook Ave			31305-	08	3	cat	—	
	0950	Abraham	2105 SW 67 Ter				09	1	Svc	12	√/6
	1050	Harris	17937 Krasnoyarsk				13	4	"	12	√/6
	1142	Cortez	8540 Williamsburg Way				14	1	"	12	√/⑥

Fig. 10- Reconciled Daily Report

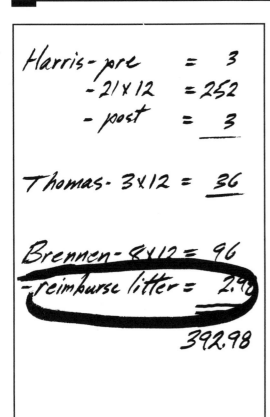

Fig.11- Deposit Receipt

your books in a few minutes. Notice it's not all revenue. You could post from money receipts, but you'll need complete information on deposit receipts, later, if you have to investigate checkbook errors. Take a moment to show on the back of the receipt what the deposit represents.

Let's finish preparing your Service Kit for tomorrow. Make sure you paperclipped tomorrow's bank deposit to the left pocket. Take your Monthly Schedule and write out a Daily Schedule, as you did today's. Then pull additional Service Agreements you'll need from where they're "suspended" in "Monthly Schedules, Pending." Place them in the left pocket with today's ongoing working copies. Replenish your supplies of fliers, pay envelopes and business cards. Except for client keys and your Daily Report clipboard, you're ready for tomorrow.

Back to the office routine; it's time to post revenue and expenditures to the books.

Since you'll do business on a "cash basis," you'll record revenue and expenses as "the money changes hands"; i.e., as you make deposits or write checks. Depending on how involved you want to get in your year-end tax accounting, your "books" can consist of sophisticated ledgers or a simple Monthly Accounting Report, as we use.

Your Monthly Accounting Report (use our forms or a commercial version available from an office supply store) gives you an account structure for grouping and tracking similar expenses ("advertising," "auto," "office supplies," etc.), and it offers columns for recording:

• daily expenditures

• daily revenue receipts, and

• expenses grouped by accounts at month-end.

Receipts *Feb 99* Expenses	Expenses (cont.) *Feb 99* Summary

(Handwritten Monthly Accounting Report form — receipts and expenses ledger with columns for Date, From, Amt, Chk. No., Paid To, Acct. No., Amt, and a Summary of expense accounts: Advertising, Auto Usage, Business Shows, Books-Magazines, Dues, Insurance, Licenses, Office Exp, Postage, Professional-Acctg, Professional-Legal, Salary, Sales Promotion, Supplies for Services, Taxes-FICA, Taxes-Medicare, Taxes-FUTA, Taxes-St. Unemployment, Taxes-Local, Telephone, and a Cash Reconciliation / Profit (Loss) section.)

Fig. 12- Monthly Accounting Report (shown full size overleaf)

The Monthly Accounting Report also helps you calculate month-end profit and track expenses, revenue and profit year-to-date.

Updating monthly records

To update your Monthly Report each day, first post your expenditures. Enter each check you've written and identify its expense with the appropriate account number. Some checks, like one closing out an Expense Report, will include several expense items, to be posted to different accounts. This entry requires more than one line, each identified by an account number (see Fig. 13).

After posting checks, place their copies, in sequence, in an envelope in your "Banking" file.

Next, post any deposits you made today. Record service fees as revenue, and show clients' names. If a deposit included a client's reimbursement for your out-of-pocket expenses (e.g. dog food or a veterinarian's fee), do not include this amount in your revenue entry. Instead, subtract it and show it as a credit to the appropriate expense account (see Fig. 14).

This posting of deposits which include a client's expense

Receipts *Feb 99*   # Expenses

Date	From	Amt.	Date	Chk. No.	Paid To	Acct. No.	Amt.
2/02	Brown	12 00	2/01	101	Fasprint	01	138 40
09	Cortez, Abraham	174 00	01	102	Ace Office Supply	08	31 10
10	Cortez	12 00	03	103	Central Check Printing	08	23 98
18	Morris	96 00	05	104	Feline Magazine	04	17 97
21	Alexander	120 00	01	ER 99-01	USPS	09	25 00
23	Harris, Thomas Brennen	390 00	03	105	Western Pet	14	11 96
28	Wentworth, Jessop	336 00	06		Valley Food Mart	13	4 15
30	Kattov, Fast	420 00	07		mileage	02	28 32
			09	106	City of Riverdale	07	30 00
			12	ER 99-02	Western Pet	14	8 98
			14	107	mileage	02	50 40
			21	ER 99-03	Valley Food Mart	13	3 88
			21	108	mileage	02	49 20
			24	109	Ace Office Supply	08	12 25
			23	depos.	Brennen reimburse litter	14	(2 98)
			28	ER 99-04	mileage	02	54 12
				110			
TOTAL THIS MONTH		1560 00					
TOTAL THROUGH LAST MONTH		-0-					
TOTAL YEAR-TO-DATE		1560 00			**TOTAL (or continue next page)**		488 73

Expenses (cont.) *FEB 99*   Summary

Date	Chk. No.	Paid To	Acct. No.	Amt.	Expense Acct.	Acct. No.	Total This Month	Total thru Last Month	Total YTD
					Advertising	1	138 40	-0-	138 40
					Auto Usage	2	182 04		182 04
					Business Shows	3			
					Books, Magazines	4	17 97		17 97
					Dues	5			
					Insurance	6			
					Licenses	7	30 00		30 00
					Office Exp.	8	69 33		69 33
					Postage	9	25 00		25 00
					Professional - Acctg.	10			
					Professional - Legal	11			
					Salary	12			
					Sales Promotion	13	8 03		8 03
					Supplies for Services	14	17 96		17 96
					Taxes - FICA	15			
					Taxes - Medicare	16			
					Taxes - FUTA	17			
					Taxes - St. Unemployment	18			
					Taxes - Local	19			
					Telephone	20			
						21			
						22			
						23			
						24			
						25			
						26			
						27			
						28			
						29			
						30			

Total This Month	488 73	
Total Through Last Month		-0-
Total Year-to-Date		488 73

CASH RECONCILIATION		PROFIT (LOSS)	Current Month	Year-to-Date
Checkbook Beginning Balance	500 00	Total Receipts	1560 00	1560 00
+ Profit (-Loss)	1071 27	(Less Expenses)	(488 00)	(488 00)
= Checkbook Ending Balance ✓	1571 27	Profit (Loss)	1071 27	1071 27

Date	Chk. No.	Paid To	Acct. No.	Amt.
2/01	101	Easprint	01	138 40
01	102	Ace Office Supply	08	31 10
03	103	Central Check Printing	08	25 98
05	104	Feline Magazine ✓	04	17 97
01	ER 99-01	USPS	09	25 00
05	105	Western Pet	14	11 96
06		Valley Food Mart	13	4 15
07	✓	mileage	02	28 32
09	106	City of Riverdale	07	30 00
12	ER 99-02	Western Pet	14	8 98
14	107	mileage	02	50 40
21	ER 99-03	Valley Food Mart	13	3 88
21	108	mileage	02	49 20
24	109	Ace Office Supply	08	12 25
23	depos.	Brennen reimburse litter	14	(2 98)
28	ER 99-04	mileage	02	54 12

Fig. 13- Monthly Accounting Report Showing Expense Checks #105, 107 and 108, closing out 3 expense reports.

Date	Chk. No.	Paid To	Acct. No.	Amt.
07	✓	mileage	02	28 32
09	106	City of Riverdale	07	30 00
12	ER 99-02	Western Pet	14	8 98
14	107	mileage	02	50 40
21	ER 99-03	Valley Food Mart	13	3 88
21	108	mileage	02	49 20
24	109	Ace Office Supply	08	12 25
23	depos.	Brennen reimburse litter	14	(2 98)
28	ER 99-04	mileage	02	54 12
	110			

Fig. 14. Posting of Deposit Including Expense Reimbursement

reimbursement is an easy opportunity for error. Having clients' payment information on the back of deposit receipts helps prevent or resolve bookkeeping errors. After posting deposits (revenue and reimbursements), file deposit receipts, sequentially by date, in "Banking."

This completes your daily bookkeeping. If you do it each day, it takes just a few minutes and makes it easy to "close out the books" at month-end.

With your service records and books caught up, let's shift to "new business." First, service your phone calls. If your answering machine or voice mail has a remote access feature, you probably retrieved and returned your calls through the day. If not, do it now. Returning calls promptly is an important part of your service reputation. And if a call requires some action, like mailing a flier, do it today.

Next, go through today's mail. Stamp all

checks for deposit, and add them to tomorrow's banking. Don't forget to complete a money receipt, mail the client's copy, then reconcile revenue with your "Hold for Payment" file. If you choose not to pay today's bills, yet, suspense them in "Accounts Payable." Review that file daily to monitor "payment due" dates and pay bills as appropriate. An alternative is to put unpaid bills into a desktop "To-Do" file in which you hold "action" or follow-up items. Again, service your To-Do file every day. Each time you pay a bill:

Handling your "To-Do" file

• study it, first, to be sure it's correct,

• post the expenditure to your Monthly Accounting Report,

• file the check copy in "Banking" and

• mark your bill copy "paid" and file in "Invoices Paid."

You'll soon start receiving business-related junk mail. Review it before throwing it away. Brochures for paper supplies or Christmas cards could come in handy later. If so, file them in "Office Supplies" and "Marketing."

Finally, if you elect to use a working To-Do file, make sure you go through it each day and take action as necessary. Your To-Do file usually should be nearly empty. If it's not, then you're either procrastinating or not using your filing system correctly.

This has been a reasonable portrayal of a pet sitter's daily office routine. Clearly, there's more to the business than caring for animals and homes. If a pet sitter is to fulfill his responsibilities, then he must have the tools and routine it takes to stay organized, day-to-day.

It doesn't have to be difficult. These procedures seem cumbersome, spread over several pages, but using them takes less time. And it gets easier the second, third and each successive time. After a few days, you'll complete each day's office routine in just a few minutes.

Unless you hire employees and have payroll responsibilities, there is no weekly routine beyond what you do daily. If you have a payroll, consult your accountant. Get his help in determining payroll requirements in your state and developing procedures which suit your business.

Month-End Routine

Closing the books

Your month-end office routine consists of "closing out the books" for the month. The idea is to conclude the month's finances, then calculate profit (or loss). First, complete your current Expense Report with entries for the last day of the month. Issue a check, post its expenses, then file the completed Expense Report and check copy. Post any other checks not yet recorded. With all expenditures during the month posted, add up account totals. Add monthly totals to prior-months' for year-to-date totals.

Record any deposits not yet posted, then add up total revenue for the month. Add this to prior months' revenue for year-to-date total revenue. Calculate profit (or loss) by subtracting total expenses from total revenue, for the month and for year-to-date. How did you do? Was it a good month? How does it compare to last month, same-month-last-year and to a year-to-date monthly average?

Reconcile your Monthly Accounting Report to your checkbook bank balance:

> does month's   checkbook beginning balance
> plus   <u>profit</u>
> equal   checkbook ending balance?

If not, then either your Monthly Report or checkbook contains at least one error.

Next, carry your year-to-date expenses and revenue over to next month's Report. You'll add next month's figures to these to calculate new year-to-date totals.

Set up other new records for planning, organizing and recording next month's activities:

• Monthly Schedule (you've probably already done this to accommodate earlier bookings for next month),

• Daily Reports and

• Expense Reports.

Your monthly bank statement probably won't arrive until early next month. Be sure to reconcile it. Having reconciled your monthly bookkeeping to your checkbook would not have revealed a common error (like recording a check for the wrong amount).

With employees, you may have monthly or at least quarterly payroll responsibilities. Consult your accountant.

Year-End Routine

Your year-end routine closes out finances for the year and for tax purposes. Depending on your legal business form, this could be a lot more complicated than calculating profit. We suggest you use your accountant for year-end accounting and tax preparation.

Another reminder -- don't let these routines scare you. They don't have to be difficult or take a lot of time. They'll guide you, keeping you organized and on track. They even can be fun -- honest!

"I don't know -- it just seems like there's a lot of duplication, like having the Service Agreement, Monthly Schedule and Daily Report all in the 'Hold for Payment' file."

Don't think of it as duplication. Realize, instead, that this routine gives you:

• A series of checks and double-checks so you don't overlook anything important and

• ready access to related records so you can detect and correct errors quickly.

These features hold your daily office routine together and make it work for you.

And now, you're actually going to do some pet sitting!

5

Providing Service

What is "Service?"

Service is the purpose and heart of your pet sitting business. Your clients don't care that you're well organized and run a business efficiently; they come to you for quality care for their pets and homes. The higher your service's quality, the more clients you'll attract and keep.

Your service is a carefully-practiced routine -- a sequence of actions, performed to satisfy clients' needs and expectations. What characterizes your routine and distinguishes it from other pet sitters' is your style. Style begins with your ethic (how you feel about animals, what you're doing and hard work) and is guided by your growing list of experiences.

Service is routine... and style

The forms your service takes are pre-service, basic service and post-service.

Pre-service, as we've discussed, allows opportunity:

• for you, the client and his pets to meet and get to know one another;

• to firm up arrangements, go over instructions and complete the Service Agreement and

• for you to get the client's key. Try the key in the door to make sure it works.

During pre-service visits, always show affection for the pets and special interest in their needs.

Post-service usually involves new clients who haven't committed, yet, to future service and letting you keep their key. It entails returning the key and collecting payment, if not already mailed. Post-service also is a marketing opportunity -- it allows you to call on the client, insure his satisfaction and convince him he'll need you in the future.

Basic service is the routine which provides for the needs of the client's pets and home while he's away. He's entrusted you with a lot of responsibility. Meeting his expectations requires you to have a plan of action -- activities sequenced into a routine. If you always follow its consecutive steps, you'll overlook nothing. Discipline yourself to practice your routine and make it second nature. If it's logical and simple, it will be easier with each new visit.

The Basic Service Routine

Your service will vary with the needs of different animals and homes, but you should follow your routine during every visit. Its sequence of steps is the framework for your service. When you must deviate for special needs (e.g., giving the dog pills or finding the rabbit which opened its cage), return to your routine so you can pick up where you left off. Just as an airline pilot uses checklists so he overlooks nothing, you should consider writing your routine on a card and carrying it until it becomes second nature. Here's the sequence which works for us:

The routine... step by step

1   Be sure to wear appropriate pet sitter's clothing -- professional-looking but functional. Since you'll have contact with many animals, anything dressy or requiring dry cleaning won't do. Your clothes should be comfortable and easy to clean. Nice jeans and simple tee shirts or sweatshirts are acceptable and more reasonable than expensive, custom-made uniforms. As a compromise, you might explore having your logo or business name imprinted on your shirts.

It's essential that your pants have a right and a left pocket to secure keys. Use the left pocket for your car keys. Discipline yourself to put them in your left pocket as you step out of the car and leave them there till you get back into the car. (As backup, hide a duplicate key in a magnetic box somewhere under your car.) Place clients' keys on the ring of a high-quality key chain or key "retriever." It must have a loop on its other end, too, so you can pass your pants belt through it. Then, secure the ring with keys in your right pocket. Should a key come off the ring, it will remain in your right pocket instead of ... who knows where! Securing keys in this fashion is vital, so you don't misplace one or lock it in the client's home as you leave.

Securing keys

2   Besides your Service Kit and its paperwork, you may need a few tools for some visits. To transport accessories, buy a small, washable nylon or canvas totebag. Provision it with:

Totebag provisions

- tape for encoding clients' keys,

- extra pens and

- a can opener.

The totebag offers extra room for carrying your Service Kit, your Daily Report clipboard between office and car and any accessories you may need from your car.

3   Check to see that your car trunk contains tools you'll need to deal with surprises or emergencies:

**In the car...
for surprises and
emergencies**

- 2 or more pooper scoopers,

- a dustpan and brush,

- a scrub brush and container of carpet cleaner (mild, safe to use and recommended for removing pet stains and odors),

- a working flashlight (check it!),

- a pet carrier and

- area maps.

To insure you're ready for any marketing opportunity, you also should have a large supply of fliers and business cards.

4   As your car engine warms before leaving the office, record today's beginning mileage on your Daily Report. Then, as you arrive at each successive stop, record the time, mileage, location and purpose. Back in the office, you'll use the mileage to update your expense report.

5   Arriving at your client's home:

Arrival at the client's home

    a. grab your totebag and lock your car;

    b. do a quick security check of the yard, looking for obvious signs of intrusion or damage. If you see any, don't enter the house -- retreat and call for police help. If all looks okay;

    c. pick up mail and newspaper. Carry them in your totebag so you have a free hand, and

    d. look at the client's Service Agreement in your Service Kit and locate the access code to his security system.

6   Remove your key ring from your right pocket, identify the client's key(s) and unlock the door. Then,

Stepping inside

    a. before opening it, lower your totebag to block the escape of pets. Carefully follow your totebag through the partly-opened door, watching for pets.

    b. Close and lock the door, go to the security panel and de-activate the alarm and

    c. at an appropriate location, sort into 3 stacks:

        - first-class mail,

        - newspapers and

        - other (catalogs, etc.).

7   Access and review the Service Agreement for pet descriptions and special instructions.

8   Locate all pets and make sure none is sick or injured. If there is a problem, check your Service Agreement and consider a trip to the client's veterinarian. Unless it appears that time is critical, finish this visit before making that trip.

9   Begin pet care with what we call the "BIG 4":

The "BIG 4"

       a. FOOD,

       b. FRESH WATER,

       c. RELIEF (potty opportunity for dogs, cleaning
          kitties' litterboxes) and

       d. AFFECTION.

Beyond the client's instructions, always:

**Always, always,
always...**

• wash bowls before the next feeding;

• feed animals only prescribed amounts;

• change water with every visit (and let the tap run for
  a minute, first, in case there's rust in the pipes);

• clean litterboxes and change the litter as necessary
  so Fluff won't judge it too dirty and use the dining
  room carpet instead and

• talk to the pets. Yours is the only voice they'll hear
  for several days.

10   After you use and tidy the kitchen counter, and while you're still in a cleaning mood, patrol all open rooms for furballs and other accidents. This is a good time to make your inside security check.

Look for:

Security check

    a. damage,

    b. signs of intrusion,

    c. anything that's different from your last visit (e.g. lights, doors, furniture placement) and

    d. hazards (we've found irons not turned off).

If you can fix a problem safely, then do so. But if there's danger, like signs of an intruder, then leave the house and call for help -- immediately!

11 Continue your home care with watering indoor plants and providing other services agreed to in the Service Agreement.

12 Be observant and correct any messes you make or find (water running from an over-watered plant, a vase knocked over by racing kitties).

13 Now the fun part -- spend time with the pets. It's important to remember that their welfare depends, not just on food and water, but on lots of attention and love, too. Talk softly and caringly to them; here's where baby talk is a professional skill! Learning to trust you, even shy kitties come out from under the bed after a visit or two. Pet, brush and play with the animals, like their owners do. Animals have all the emotions we do, including jealousy, so don't favor or slight one over another. As you play with them, be sure they get some exercise. For dogs, you've discussed with the client short walks or access to the back yard. Cats love to chase toys or string, and that's good exercise. Just be careful not to over-exercise them or leave toys which could hurt them.

The fun part

14 When you've given reasonable time to the pets (remember to watch the time) and think you've completed service, access your Service Kit and review the Service Agreement carefully. Forget anything? Don't skip this step.

15   Now write a daily note if you've decided it's appropriate. Some clients love to read daily notes about their pets, your visits, and even the weather while they were away. Others feel that writing notes takes time away from their pets; they'd rather you spend the time loving and playing with the animals. As you learn to 'read' your clients, you'll be able to judge how they feel about daily notes. If you're not sure, ask them. Sometimes a single note, left on the last visit, is adequate. It's also functional -- be sure it reminds the client to call you as soon as he returns home. Then you know the pets are provided for, again. When you do leave notes, make them honest and specific. Our clients enjoy notes which demonstrate we really understand their pets' personalities.

The daily note

16   Leave a pay envelope with your last-visit note. We find it prompts otherwise-slow payers. Also leave a couple business cards -- one so the client has your phone number handy and another for him to give a friend.

17   Before leaving, locate all pets, again, to insure none is closed in a room or closet.

18   Secure your totebag and make sure it contains your Service Kit and any accessories you may have brought into the home. Also check that you've removed the client's mail and newspaper from it.

Again, this sequence of activities is the framework of your service routine. But anyone can perform the sequence and still make mistakes. Performing service correctly involves some dos and don'ts. These dos and don'ts are basic rules for pet sitters and the first ingredient of your style and success. Don't forget them.

ALWAYS treat every client like he's special and your only one.

NEVER imply you're too busy or will have to "squeeze in" his service.

ALWAYS insist the client give you a key.

NEVER accept only a garage door opener. (How would you get in during a long power outage?)

ALWAYS start your day early and allow enough time for problems and ample service.

NEVER procrastinate.

ALWAYS treat all client information confidentially. Safeguard your records as you do clients' keys.

NEVER discuss clients, their plans, pets or homes.

NEVER answer a client's phone. You may unwittingly provide information to an intruder.

NEVER take another person (except an employee) into a client's home.

ALWAYS treat the clients' pets and homes as you would your own. But ...

ALWAYS provide service only to the extent specified in the Service Agreement.

NEVER go beyond unless circumstances (like an emergency) and good judgment suggest action.

NEVER perform unnecessary service which could offend the client (e.g., changing his brand of pet food or cleaning what you regard to be a "dirty" room).

ALWAYS avoid curiosity. You're in the house to provide care and security.

NEVER touch or access anything that isn't part of your service.

NEVER remove or "borrow" anything.

ALWAYS treat every visit like your last. Leave everything "spiffy" after each visit.

NEVER put off a service task until the next visit. There may not be one if the client comes home early.

ALWAYS expect and plan for surprises. Think about what you'll do if you encounter car trouble, damage, an intruder or injured pets.

NEVER let a client leave town without discussing emergency veterinarian care.

"Okay - a sequence of responsibilities and a list of rules - I'm ready for service!"

Almost. These will make you efficient and keep you out of trouble, but your service routine needs a third ingredient - style.

Remember that it's your style that sets you apart from others. It rounds out your service, giving your routine color, body and distinction. Your style stems from the concern you feel and the care and attention you give to each client, his pets and home. What you put into your style is energy and effort. What comes out is performance quality.

Style and Quality

Your style is completely within your control. You can cut corners and never be rebooked by that client. You can satisfy the client by doing just enough to fulfill your Service Agreement obligations. Or, you can put extra energy into each visit (believe us, it will show!) so the client is eager to plan another trip around your service. And in the meantime, he'll promote you with friends and coworkers. In short, anyone can follow instructions, but it will be your style which makes you stand out. Decide what your style will be, then start working on it.

As part of your style, you might consider client recognition and using small gifts when appropriate. We mentioned Christmas cards. During the pre-service visit, we like to leave an inexpensive

Client recognition

toy which we buy in bulk. We also leave a small fruit selection during the last visit when a client has been away for a long period. These simple expressions of our appreciation please and impress clients.

Anticipate surprises

We warned you to anticipate surprises. Give this a little more thought. Surprises involve not just clients' homes, but your problems. Car trouble is the obvious example.

"No problem. My sister isn't working -- I'll just use her car."

Are you sure it will be available? Maybe you'd better call a couple rental agencies in deciding what your contingency plan will be.

What if you become ill or must care for a sick family member? Maybe that's reason to consider having someone else involved in your business. Then there's inclement weather -- can you complete a high number of visits on Christmas Day if the streets are icy? Again, maybe you'll need help. More on "help" in the next chapter.

The point is, there are living creatures out there who will depend on you to meet their basic needs. You've got to have contingency plans!

Ah, Success!

Making sure the client is happy

Your service is successful each time a client returns home, finds it exactly as he left it and his pets as happy as if he'd never left them. But don't take for granted, just because you feel good about a client's service, that he shares your enthusiasm. You have to follow-up -- insure he is pleased or find out why not. If he fails to call to report he's home (and that "... things couldn't look better!"), then you must call him. You have the perfect excuse -- you need to know that the pets are provided for. If the client doesn't offer, ask if everything looks okay and was your service to his liking. The warm response you'll probably get is one of the big rewards of pet sitting.

This follow-up on your part -- guaranteeing client satisfaction -- is an important marketing tool. Why? Because it registers with the client as care and concern. He'll book you again and again. Repeat clients, involving no pre-service or post-service (when you retain their key), cost far less to serve than new clients. And they require no advertising -- they're already sold on your services. Speaking of advertising -- don't forget that satisfaction is the basis for word-of-mouth, the best advertising of all.

We've painted a pretty rosy picture of successful pet sitting, and if you use a service routine like ours, you'll almost always have happy clients. What do you do, though, if you get a complaint? First, don't let it discourage you. Most good professionals receive an occasional complaint. Deal with it quickly, honestly and fairly. Identify the client's dissatisfaction and ask what he feels would be fair remedy. Consider "comping" him (i.e., not charging for) one or more visits. Resolve the complaint, then learn from it. Learning and growing are part of your style. Finally, consider that the client's dissatisfaction may not be your fault or within your control. Maybe it's the client's problem, and you just happened to get in the way. Not all humans think and behave as we'd like them to. (Maybe that's why we like animals so much!) This leads to one last service topic.

Dealing with complaints

Speaking of mistakes and learning from them, allow us to suggest that you'll meet people you'd rather not have as clients. We have. In two instances, repeat clients who constantly praised and tried to befriend us turned cold when we politely refused their requests to teach them our business. One became threatening. We promptly returned their keys! Others we've met seem to enjoy sharing their misfortune or unhappiness. There's little a pet sitter can do to help these folks, but you can help yourself by avoiding them. Your business doesn't need fictitious complaints or bogus claims against it. As you learn to judge character, you'll sense when a would-be booking doesn't "feel right." When you sense danger or disappointment, it's a good time to set aside time for yard work, shopping or half-day vacations; i.e., be "booked" on those dates. Don't judge too quickly, but there are times you should avoid or sever relationships which could be costly or disappointing. Remember one motive -- you're in this business to have a little fun!

Judging potential clients

Summary

To conclude our discussion about service, let's re-emphasize its important aspects. What your service should consist of are:

• a logical sequence of activities -- the framework of your routine,

• a list of rules -- dos and don'ts -- which guide you within your routine and grows with your experience and

• your style -- the attitudes, effort and characteristics which set your performance apart from others.

What will make your service successful are:

• discipline,

• genuine concern and

• the will to succeed and the willingness to work for it -- your ethic.

If it's your goal to be the best pet sitter around, then do it! You know how.

6

Pitfalls and Adjustments

"Why the Negatives?"

No instruction in starting a new business is "complete" without a discussion of its pitfalls. Why? The purpose of instruction is to get you started. Your start will be a lot quicker and smoother if you can learn from others' experiences and avoid their mistakes. To anticipate pitfalls and plan around them is to be forewarned and forearmed.

Pet sitting is a wonderful service and a fun profession, but it's not without pitfalls. Some, like working too hard, stem from your ethic -- the care and energy you'll put into your work. All pitfalls can be avoided or controlled through adjustments.

Avoiding pitfalls

We've discussed several pet sitting pitfalls already:

• underpricing your services,

• ineffective marketing,

• working long hours with no days off,

• allowing your business to dominate your personal life,

• a lack of contingency plans and

• the complications of having employees.

The first two aren't difficult to deal with -- Chapter 3 tells us how. The last four are more challenging. Notice that they all involve manpower -- having help when you need it.

More About "Help"

The "official helper"

To discuss "help" a little further, let's say you've decided it's not practical -- at least initially -- to have employees. And maybe you have good reasons for not wanting partners. Who, then, will be available to help you with service when:

• it snows a foot,

• you're too sick to get out of bed or

• you really need a short vacation.

We're lucky. Although Scott has another full-time job, he's usually available if Lori needs help. But if your business doesn't have an official helper, what can you do? As we suggested earlier, consider working with one or more friendly competitors.

"Other Pet Sitters?!"

Suppose you've tried to hold free a weekend for a <u>badly-needed mini-vacation</u>. Then, as you start to pack, a good client calls, equally desperate for service on those dates. Do you accept his booking and cancel your plans? There's an alternative. Explain your circumstances and ask if he'd consider using another pet sitter this one time -- someone you feel performs service to your standards. Anticipating the pitfall earlier, you called the sitter and found she can, indeed, "cover" you. The client agrees, and you give him the pet sitter's phone number or -- better -- you have her call him. Everyone's happy, and you'll cover the other sitter when she needs your help.

You can also ask her help in a <u>personal emergency</u>, as when you're sick or injured. Realize, though, that there are liability issues, here, because the client's contract is with you, and he thinks you're performing all service. The way to avoid problems is to discuss emergencies and contingency plans with the client as you complete the Service Agreement. In fact, you may want to address contingencies in your Agreement.

Certainly, there can be pitfalls in selecting other pet sitters to help you. Besides adequate service and liability issues, you don't want to lose clients to competitors. If you have a choice, get help from pet sitters who live just beyond your service areas -- so that serving your clients is business they ordinarily wouldn't solicit.

Is it unnatural to cooperate with other pet sitters? Not if it benefits you. Consider that you may be more <u>help</u> than threat to one another (especially if you work far enough apart so that you don't really "compete"). One sitter's advertising, for example, often helps others by promoting pet sitting in general. And getting together to swap tales and discuss problems is a great way to pick up tips and new techniques. Most important, other pet sitters -- who you know work as professionally as you -- are a source of help when you need it.

Other Pitfalls

Another pitfall involving your service capacity is the <u>good client who calls late -- when you're already booked solid</u>. This usually occurs during your busiest periods, like Christmas and spring break. What's different is the adjustment. You don't want to risk losing a "preferred client," so you won't refer him to another pet sitter. What can you do? One alternative is to "overbook" - commit to one more visit per day than you'd like to make. And, if there's a cancellation, then you're no longer over-booked. Another adjustment -- having anticipated the problem -- is to communicate with preferred clients well before busy periods. Use phone calls and early Christmas cards to encourage them to consider their plans and book with you early, while you're still available. This kind of planning makes excellent use of your time during the slow periods we discussed in Chapter 3.

Encourage early bookings

Speaking of the telephone, you may find yourself having longer and longer conversations with good clients. While these help build relationships, too much phone time keeps you in the office and postpones your service routine. The adjustment involves watching the time and developing important telephone techniques. Teach and force yourself to conduct your business, visit quickly, then politely end your phone call so you can continue with today's schedule.

A good reason to spend time on the phone is insuring you understand the client's instructions and his service needs. You vaguely remember him mentioning medication, but you didn't ask questions when you should have. Now he's begun his cruise, and you don't know which cat gets the pills. And it looks like the ivy is dying -- you should have asked how he cares for it! Be sure you probe during pre-service visits, and telephone later, if necessary, to get all the information you'll need.

Search out a "technical advisor"

There will be some problems -- surprises -- which clients' instructions won't address. What do you do if you find a broken water pipe? You don't want to call the fire department, but you're not sure just how to control this situation. Inadequate technical background is a pitfall. Your adjustment involves finding out, in advance, where you can get technical advice. Maybe your father-in-law or Jacob, the retired school janitor who lives next door, would gladly help you with technical emergencies.

As you fine-tune your routines and trim steps to become more efficient, don't get into ruts. Inflexibility is a serious pitfall. Perhaps you think you don't have time to listen to Jacob's lecture about plumbing. If you do, though, you'll know how to deal with the next broken pipe you find. Force yourself to be open-minded and receptive to new ideas. You've been wasting time for months using that awkward two-sided expense report. Design a simpler one!

Let's conclude with some pitfalls involving expenses. The first involves the mileage reimbursement you take for use of your own car. You say your old bug is falling apart with all the business miles you're putting on it. But you have no money to replace it? What happened to your mileage reimbursement? Hey, that's not "income!" It's supposed to defray your gas and maintenance expenses and help pay for a new car! If driving the bug costs you, say, 7¢ per mile (gas and oil) and if you're taking, say, 26¢ per mile reimbursement, then you should be putting 19¢ per mile into a cookie jar towards a replacement car.

How come you're claiming "business lunch" and entertainment expenses each week? Are they really necessary for your business? How about the TV you bought for the office? You don't need to convince us, but consider how you'll justify these as legitimate "business expenses" if <u>the IRS audits you</u>.

Keep expenses legit

Perhaps you can justify to the IRS all your expensive office accessories, like the personal computer and its printer. But do you really need them? Avoid the <u>temptation to waste money on "toys"</u>-- accessories you don't need, yet.

With experience, you'll encounter other pitfalls -- some not worth mentioning, here, and some which we haven't discovered, yet. You'll make adjustments, and you'll make a few mistakes. That's okay, if you learn from your errors. Your challenge is to keep learning, improving and growing. To meet the challenge, you should like what you're doing. You have that opportunity with pet sitting. We hope you have as much fun with it as we do!

Keep learning, improving and growing

Professional
Pet Sitter
Forms

Client Card

Name: _____   Pets: Name, M / F, Age, Type
Address: _____   1. _____
Apt. _____   _____
City_____ State _____ Zip_____   2. _____
                                                                 _____
Phone:_____   3. _____
                                                                 _____
Referred By: _____
Vet is : _____At:_____
Phone: _____
Pet Medication: _____

Directions: _____
_____
_____

Contacts: _____
_____
_____

Service Agreement

Name: _____   Directions to Home: _____

_____   _____

Address: _____   _____

_____   _____

City:_____State ____Zip ___   _____

Home Phone: _____   Office Phone: _____Ext. _____

Name(s) and Description(s) of pet(s):
1. _____
2. _____
3. _____
4. _____
5. _____

Date Leaving_____ Time _____ Date Returning _____ Time _____

You can be reached at: _____   Phone _____

Local Emergency Contact: Name _____   Phone _____

Persons with access to your home: _____

Your Vet: Name _____Phone _____

Other services included in our fees: ❑ Mail   ❑ Paper   ❑ Alter lights
                                         ❑ Water plants   In _____ out _____
                                         ❑ Other _____

Special instructions: _____

_____

_____

Recycle cans?   ❑ Yes   ❑ No

Location of food: _____

(Company Name) _____agrees to provide services from _____ through _____ .
Total number of visits _____ at $_____ each, key pickup $ _____, key return $_____,
for a total of $_____ . Services will be performed in accordance with the instructions contained
herein. The client waives any claims against (Company Name) unless (Company Name) is negligent
and does not perform as agreed herein. Payment due upon completion. Please use the attached
envelope to mail payment on the date of your return.

For (Company Name) _____   Client _____
Date: _____   Date: _____

Daily Report

Month: _____ **19** _____

Date	Time	Name	Address	Begin	End	Total	Purp.	Rev.

Time Sheet **Name:** _____

Date	Times				Name	Address	Begin	End	Total	Purp.	Rev.
	Lv	Ar	Stay	OT							

Employee Expense Report

Week of _____

To Whom Paid	Reason For Expenditure	Acct									Totals
Mileage @											
Daily Totals											

Employee Signature _____ Date _____

Job Title _____

Supervisor's Signature _____ Date _____

Job Title _____

Total Expenses on this report _____

Add Previous balance due employee _____

New Balance due employee _____

Check # _____ Issued _____

Carry forward balance due employee _____

Receipts

Expenses

Date	From	Amt.		Date	Chk. No.	Paid To	Acct. No.	Amt.	
TOTAL THIS MONTH									
TOTAL THROUGH LAST MONTH									
TOTAL YEAR-TO-DATE					**TOTAL (or continue next page)**				

Expenses (cont.)   # Summary

Date	Chk. No.	Paid To	Acct. No.	Amt.	Expense Acct.	Acct. No.	Total This Month	Total thru Last Month	Total YTD
					Advertising	1			
					Auto Usage	2			
					Business Shows	3			
					Books, Magazines	4			
					Dues	5			
					Insurance	6			
					Licenses	7			
					Office Exp.	8			
					Postage	9			
					Professional - Acctg.	10			
					Professional - Legal	11			
					Salary	12			
					Sales Promotion	13			
					Supplies for Services	14			
					Taxes - FICA	15			
					Taxes - Medicare	16			
					Taxes - FUTA	17			
					Taxes - St. Unemployment	18			
					Taxes - Local	19			
					Telephone	20			
						21			
						22			
						23			
						24			
						25			
						26			
						27			
						28			
						29			
						30			

Total This Month

Total Through Last Month

Total Year-to-Date

CASH RECONCILIATION			PROFIT (LOSS)	Current Month	Year-to-Date
Checkbook Beginning Balance			Total Receipts		
+ Profit (-Loss)			(Less Expenses)		
= Checkbook Ending Balance			Profit (Loss)		

ORDER FORM

Do you **LOVE ANIMALS?**

Do you want to **SUPPLEMENT YOUR INCOME?**

Are you interested in a **CAREER IN PET SITTING?**

We have been providing loving in-home pet care since 1988.

Let us help **YOU** get started.

THE PROFESSIONAL PET SITTER includes:

- how to organize and run the business

- how to price and market

- the forms you will need

Mail order form and check/money order for $29.95 (postpaid within the US and Canada) to:

PAWS-ITIVE PRESS®
PO Box 19911
Portland OR 97280-0911

Add $3.20 for Priority Mail. Overseas buyers please pay by money order in US Dollars, or by draft on a US bank. Visa/MasterCard accepted. Call (800) PET BOOK or (503) 452-9699. E-mail: petbook@worldnet.att.net   http://www.bookzone.com/petsitting

Name: _____

Company: _____

Address: _____

City, State, Zip: _____

Daytime Phone: (   )_____

Total Copies Ordered: _____   Total Amount Enclosed $ _____